Exploring the MET

by Kathleen Odenthal

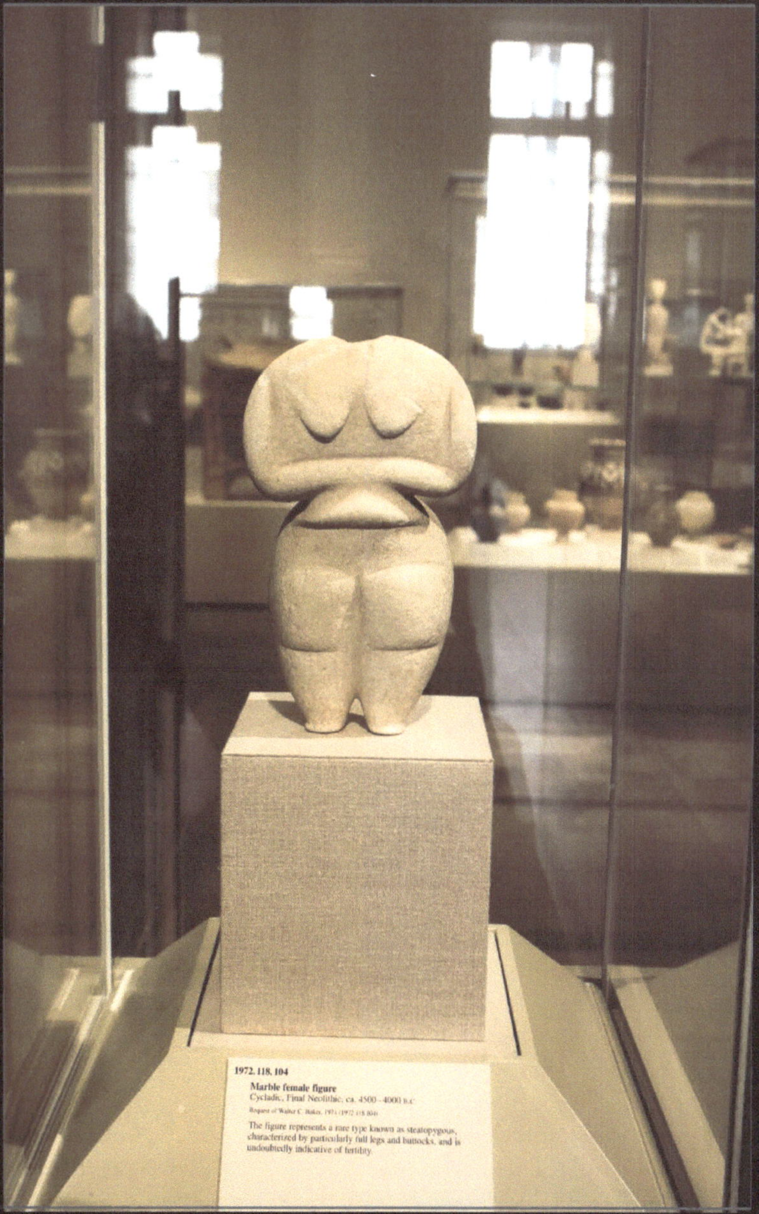

1972.118.104
Marble female figure
Cycladic, Final Neolithic, ca. 4500–4000 B.C.
Bequest of Walter C. Baker, 1971 (1972.118.104)

The figure represents a rare type known as steatopygous, characterized by particularly full legs and buttocks, and is undoubtedly indicative of fertility.

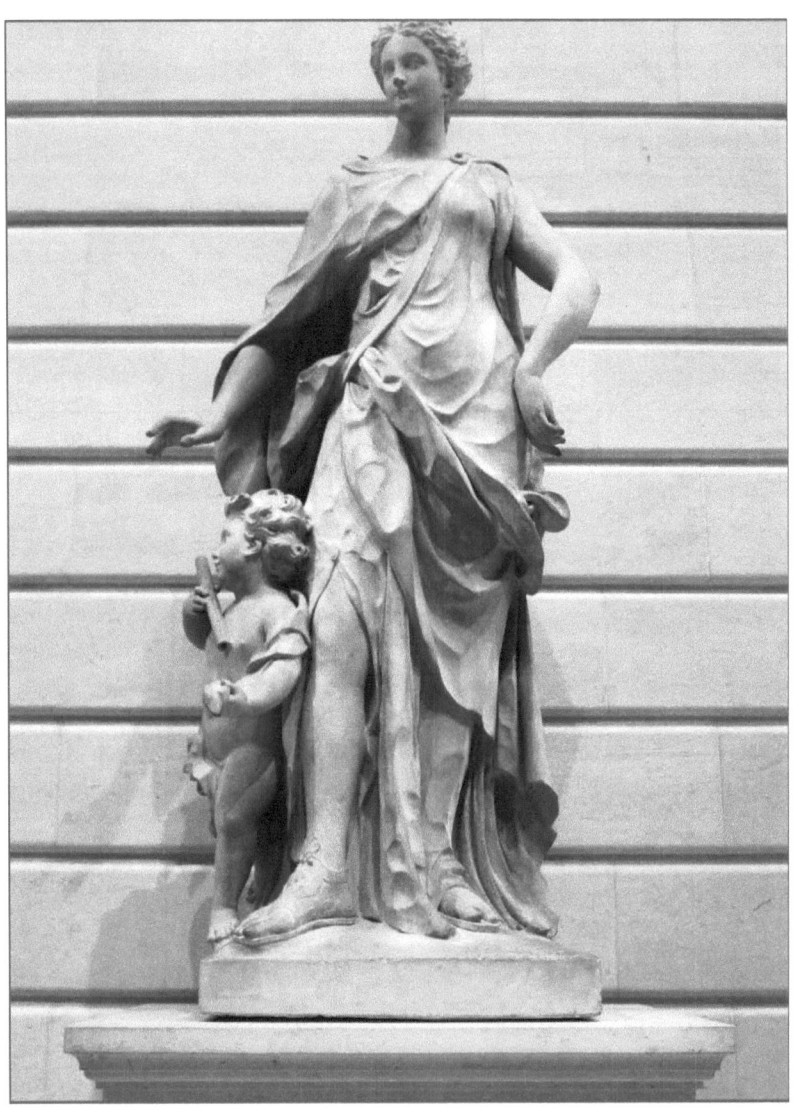

AIR

Limestone
Probably by JEAN-PIERRE DEFRANCE (1694–1768)
French (Rouen), about 1750–60

One of a series representing the Four Elements, which
stood in the park of the Château de Mussegros at Écouis,
near Rouen in Normandy.

Purchase, Charles Ulrick and Josephine Bay Foundation, Inc.
Gift, 1964
64.93.4

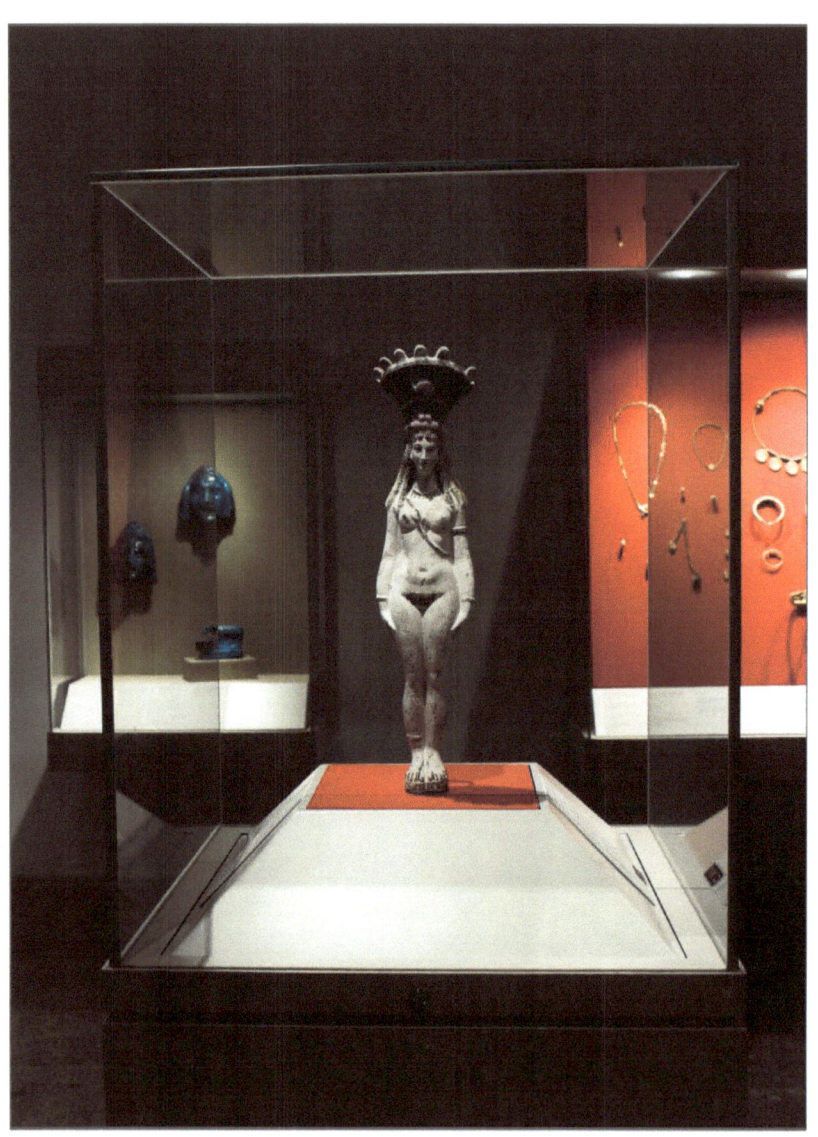

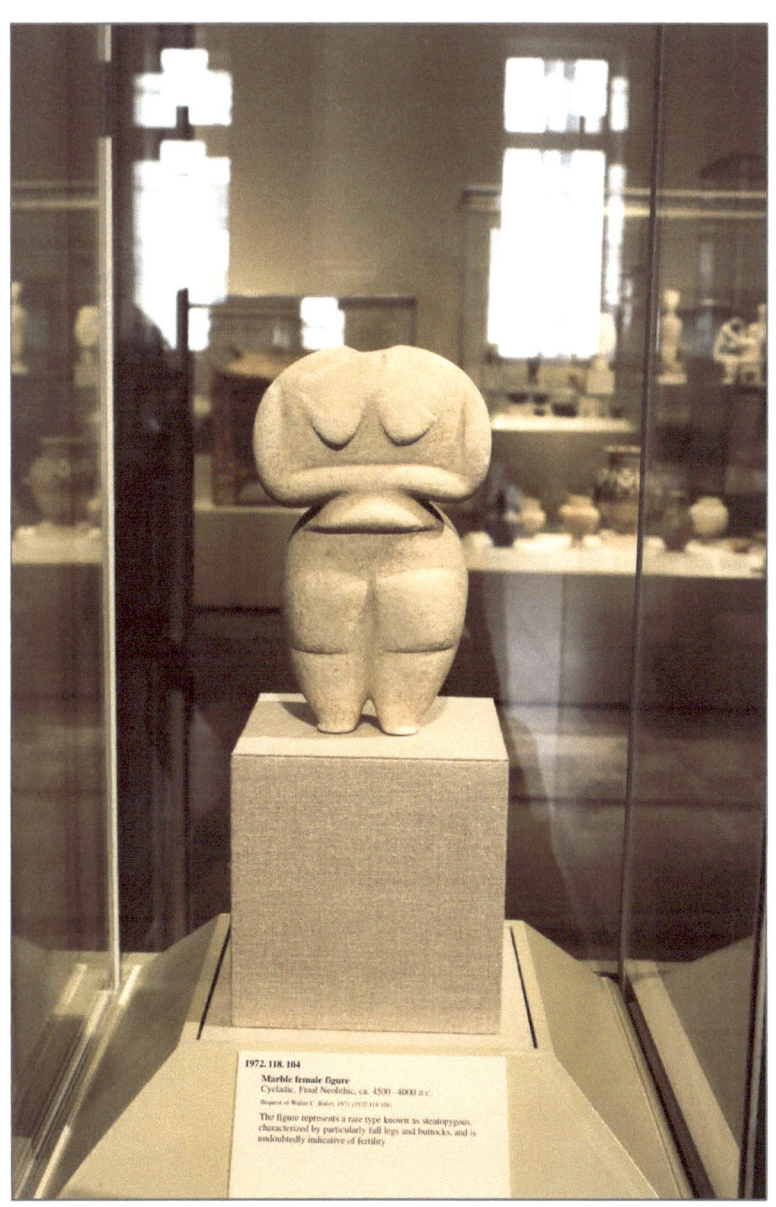

1972. 118. 104
Marble female figure
Cycladic, Final Neolithic, ca. 4500 - 4000 B.C.
Bequest of Walter C. Baker, 1971 (1972.118.104)

The figure represents a rare type known as steatopygous, characterized by particularly full legs and buttocks, and is undoubtedly indicative of fertility.

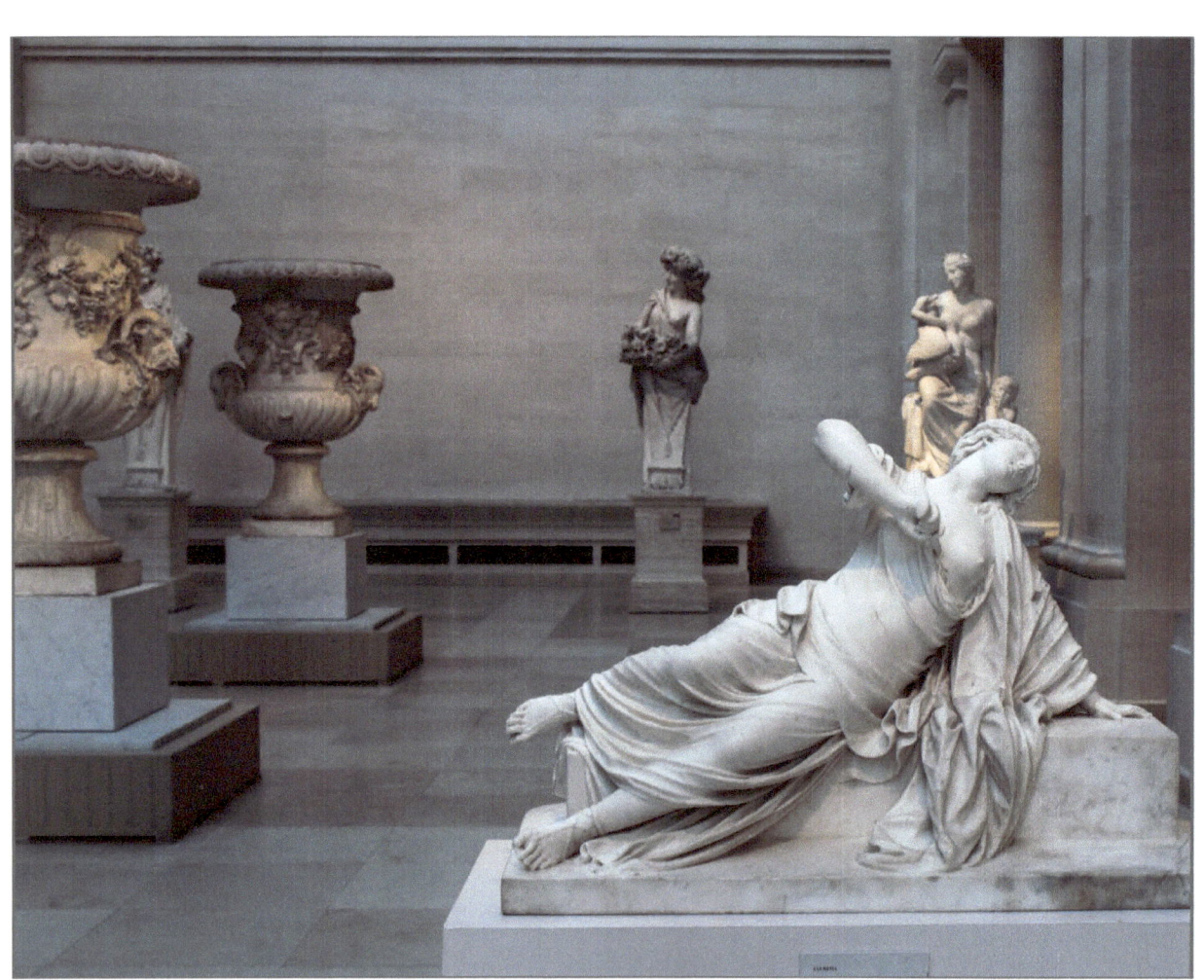

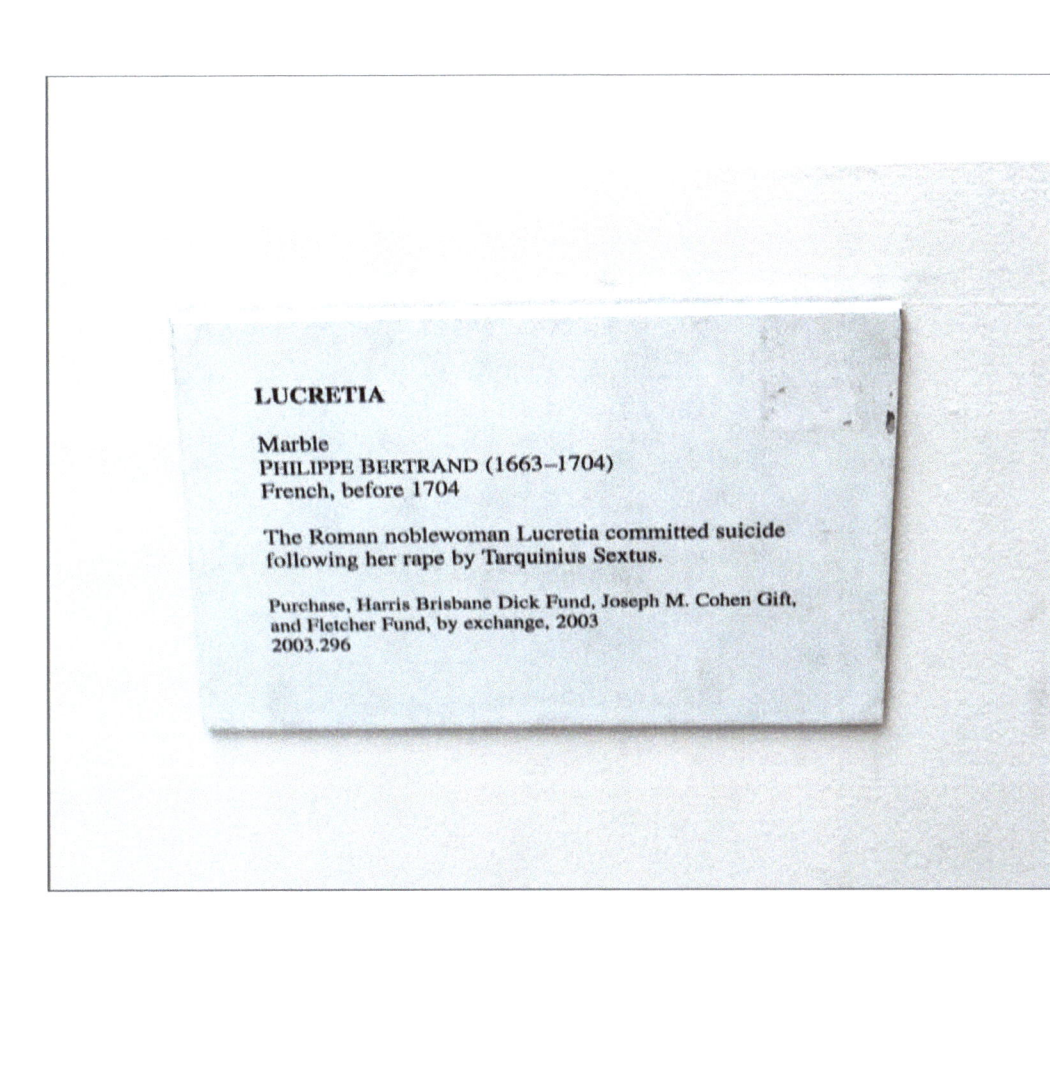

LUCRETIA

Marble
PHILIPPE BERTRAND (1663–1704)
French, before 1704

The Roman noblewoman Lucretia committed suicide
following her rape by Tarquinius Sextus.

Purchase, Harris Brisbane Dick Fund, Joseph M. Cohen Gift,
and Fletcher Fund, by exchange, 2003
2003.296

PORTRAIT OF A WOMAN (MARIANNA PANCIATICHI, MARCHESA PAOLUCCI DELLE RONCOLE, 1835–1919, OR HER SISTER-IN-LAW, BEATRICE FERRARI-CORBELLI DI REGGIO, CONTESSA DI LUCCIANO)

Oil on canvas
MICHELE GORDIGIANI (1830–1909)
Italian, 1864

Michele Gordigiani was the premier portraitist of the Risorgimento, the period of modern Italian unification. This portrait, commissioned from him by marchese Ferdinando Panciatichi (1813–1897/98), scion of a distinguished Florentine family, depicts the patron's daughter or daughter-in-law. That it was one of a pair—the pendant is now unlocated—can be deduced from the original receipt for the exuberant gilt wood frame with silk velvet elements the painting still bears, a masterpiece of the *intagliatore*, or carver, Niccola Ricci (active 1848–1866). The frame's opulence is evocative of the years from 1864 until 1871, when Florence served as King Vittorio Emmanuele II's temporary capitol.

Purchase, Anne Cox Chambers Fund, 2011
2011.9

PAIR
MAN

Gilt v
Possi

With
are r
furni

Purch
and A
1991

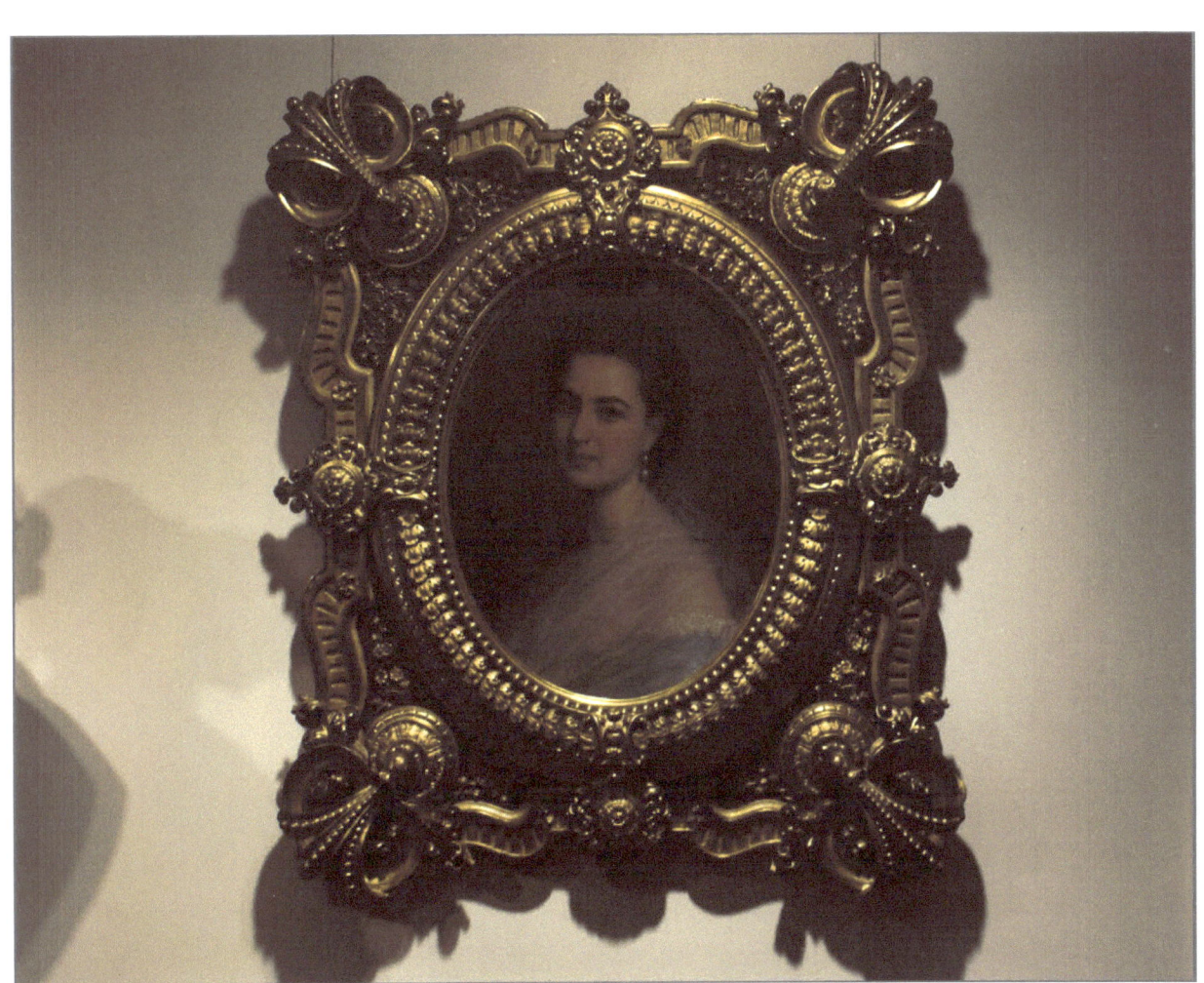

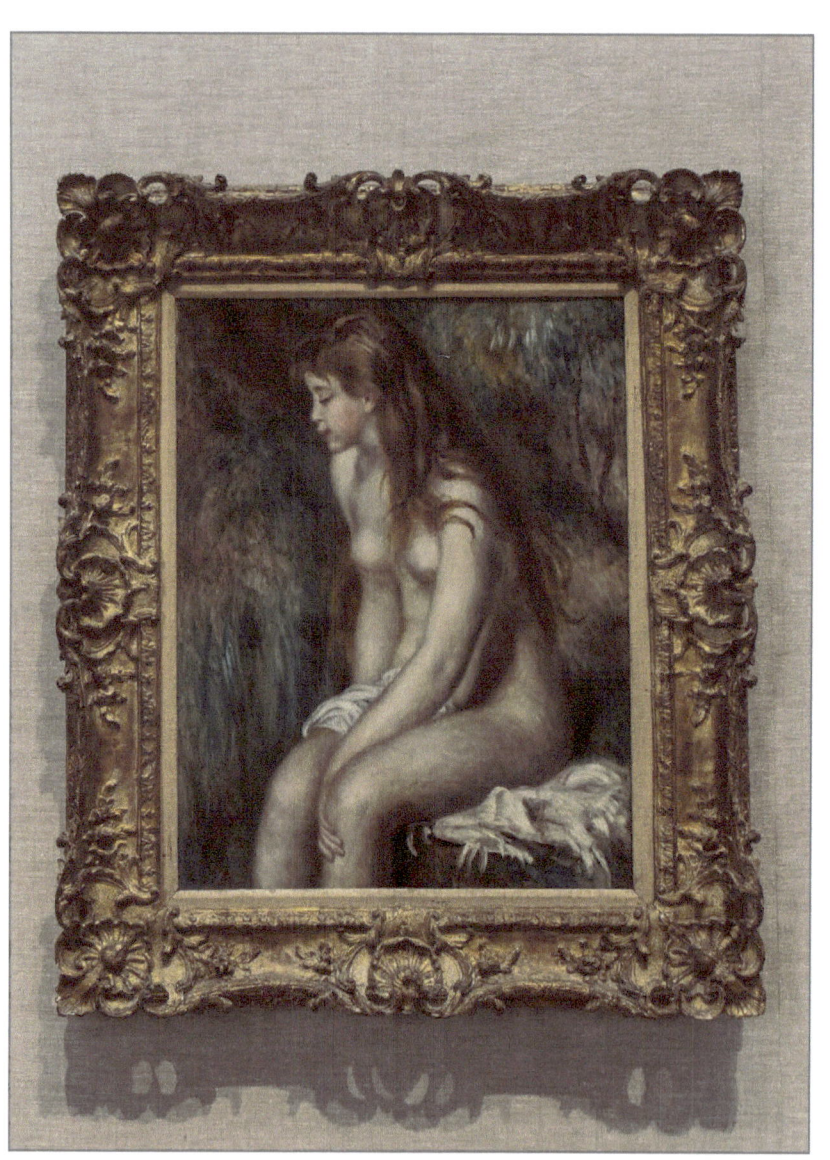

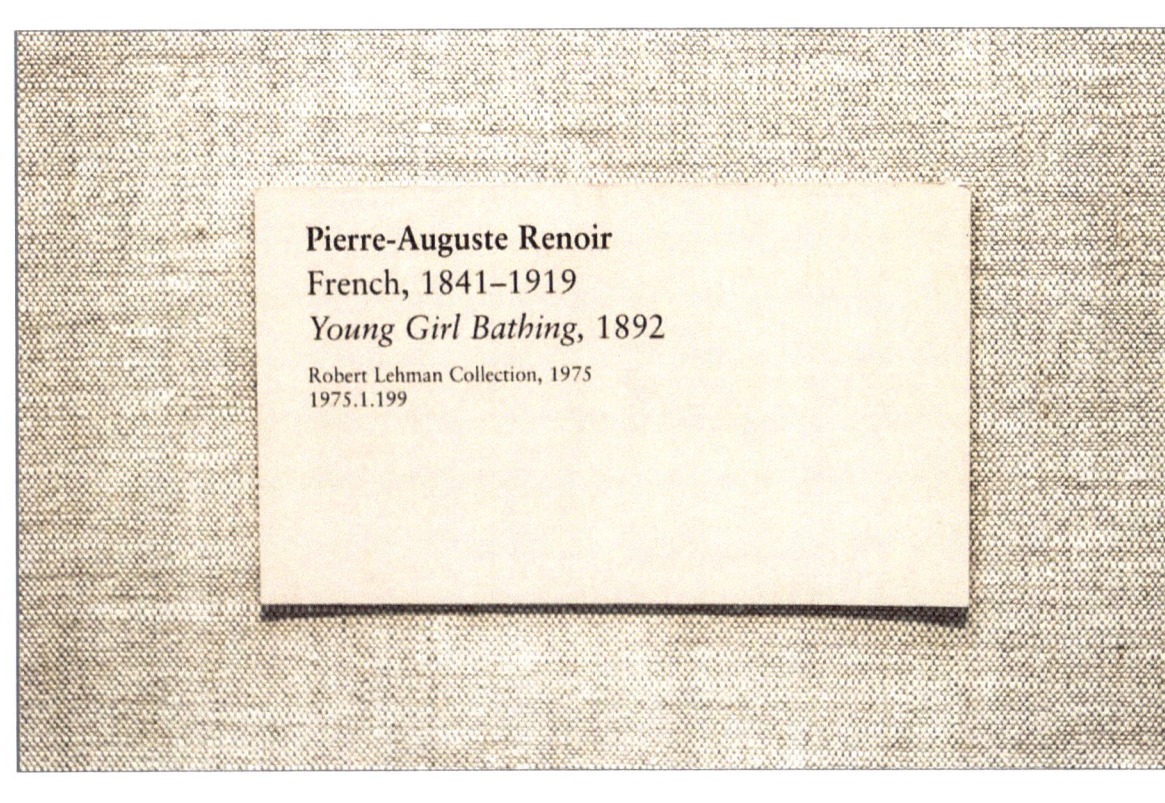

Pierre-Auguste Renoir
French, 1841–1919
Young Girl Bathing, 1892

Robert Lehman Collection, 1975
1975.1.199

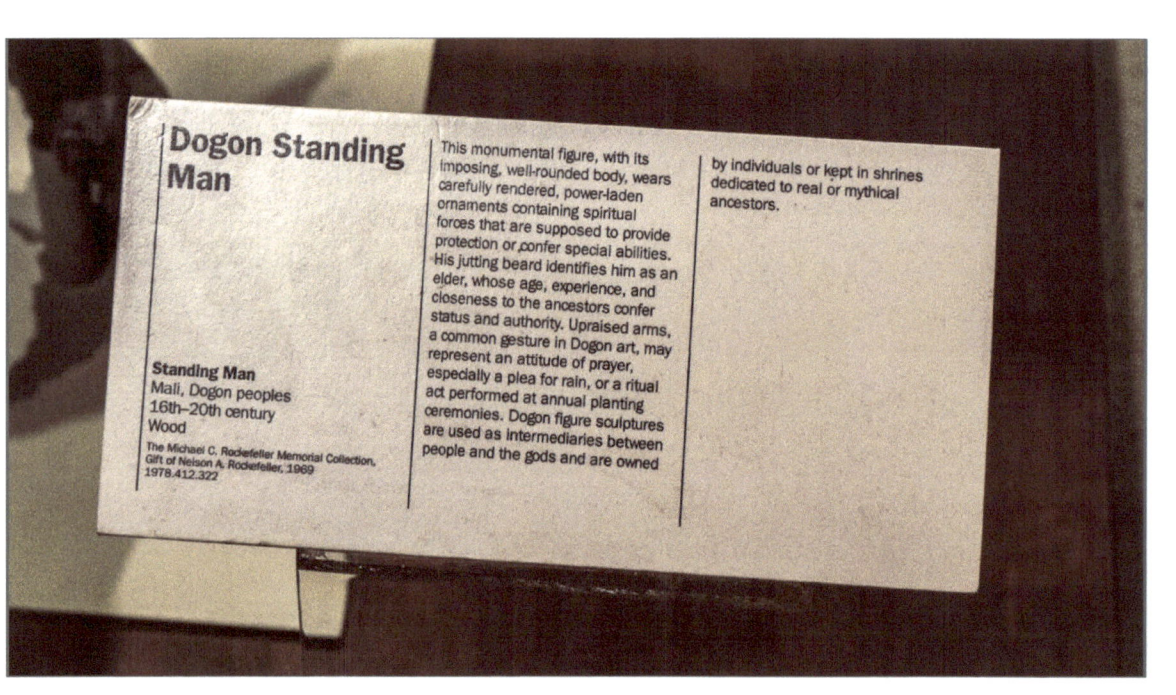

Dogon Standing Man

Standing Man
Mali, Dogon peoples
16th–20th century
Wood

The Michael C. Rockefeller Memorial Collection,
Gift of Nelson A. Rockefeller, 1969
1978.412.322

This monumental figure, with its imposing, well-rounded body, wears carefully rendered, power-laden ornaments containing spiritual forces that are supposed to provide protection or confer special abilities. His jutting beard identifies him as an elder, whose age, experience, and closeness to the ancestors confer status and authority. Upraised arms, a common gesture in Dogon art, may represent an attitude of prayer, especially a plea for rain, or a ritual act performed at annual planting ceremonies. Dogon figure sculptures are used as intermediaries between people and the gods and are owned by individuals or kept in shrines dedicated to real or mythical ancestors.

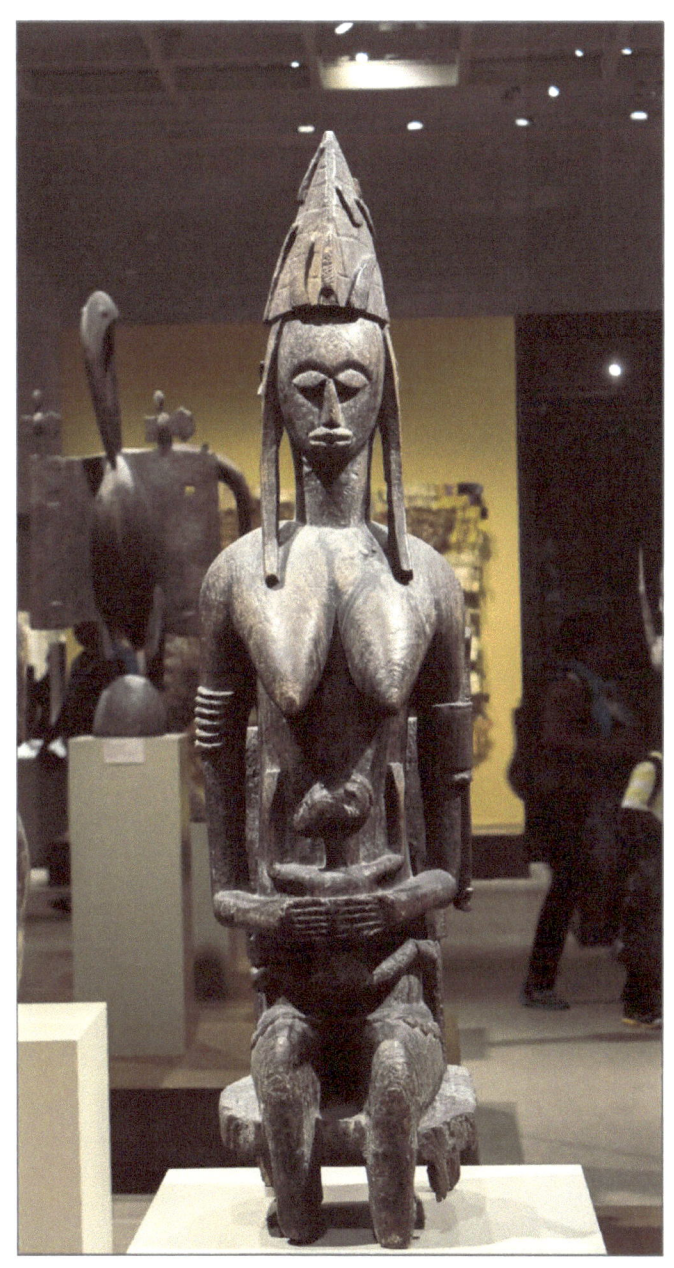

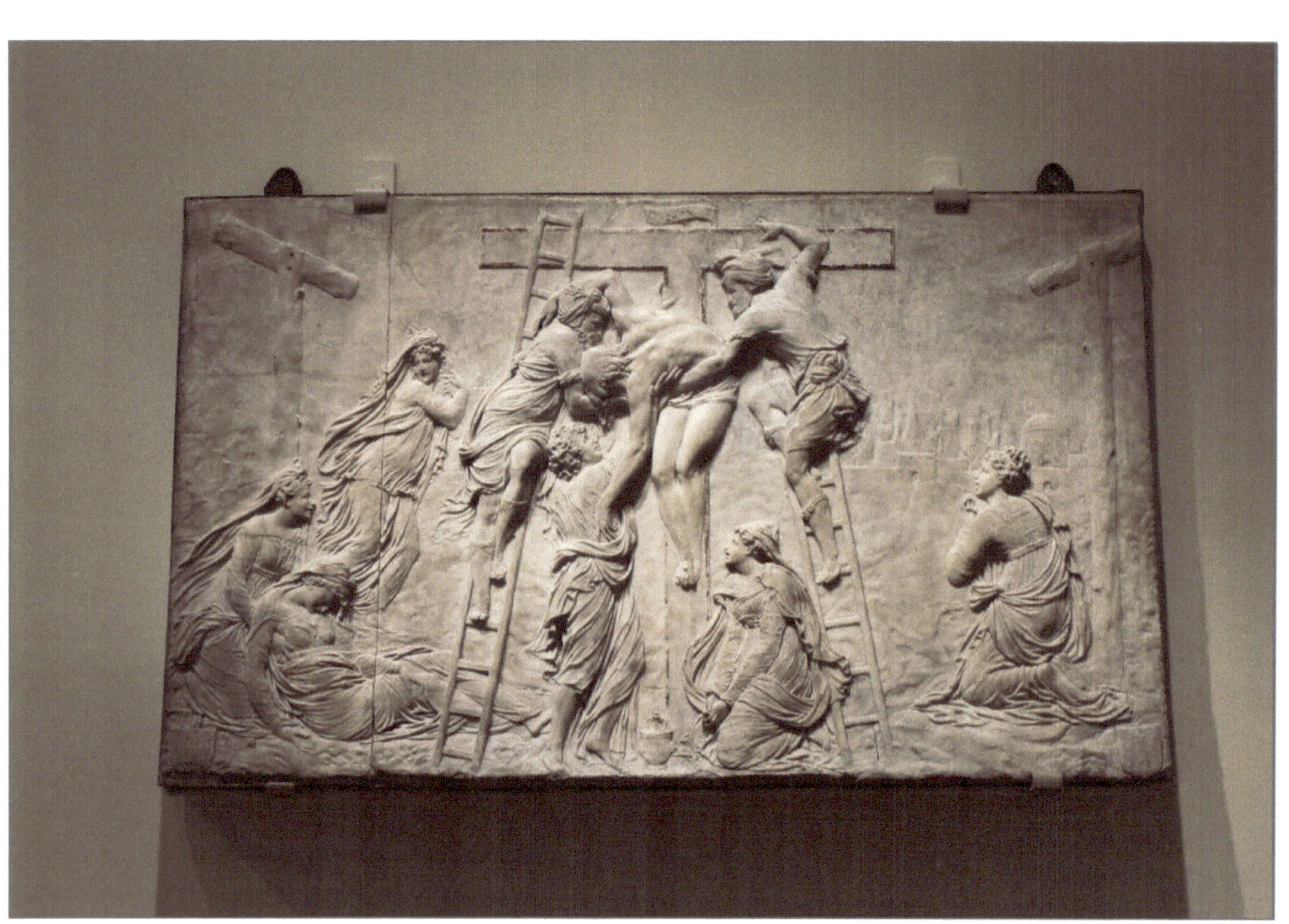

Descent from the Cross

Marble with traces of gilding
Follower of **Jean Goujon** (ca. 1510–ca. 1565)
French (Paris), ca. 1555

Against a distant view of Jerusalem, Christ's body is lowered into
the arms of Saint John the Evangelist under the anguished gaze of
Mary Magdalen, who kneels at the foot of the cross. On the left,
one of the other Maries supports the swooning Virgin. Although the
composition was based on an engraving by the Bolognese printmaker
Marcantonio Raimondi (ca. 1480–before 1534), the figures' thin
draperies, elongated silhouettes, and Grecian profiles reflect the
influence of the court artist Jean Goujon.

Fletcher Fund, 1929
29.56

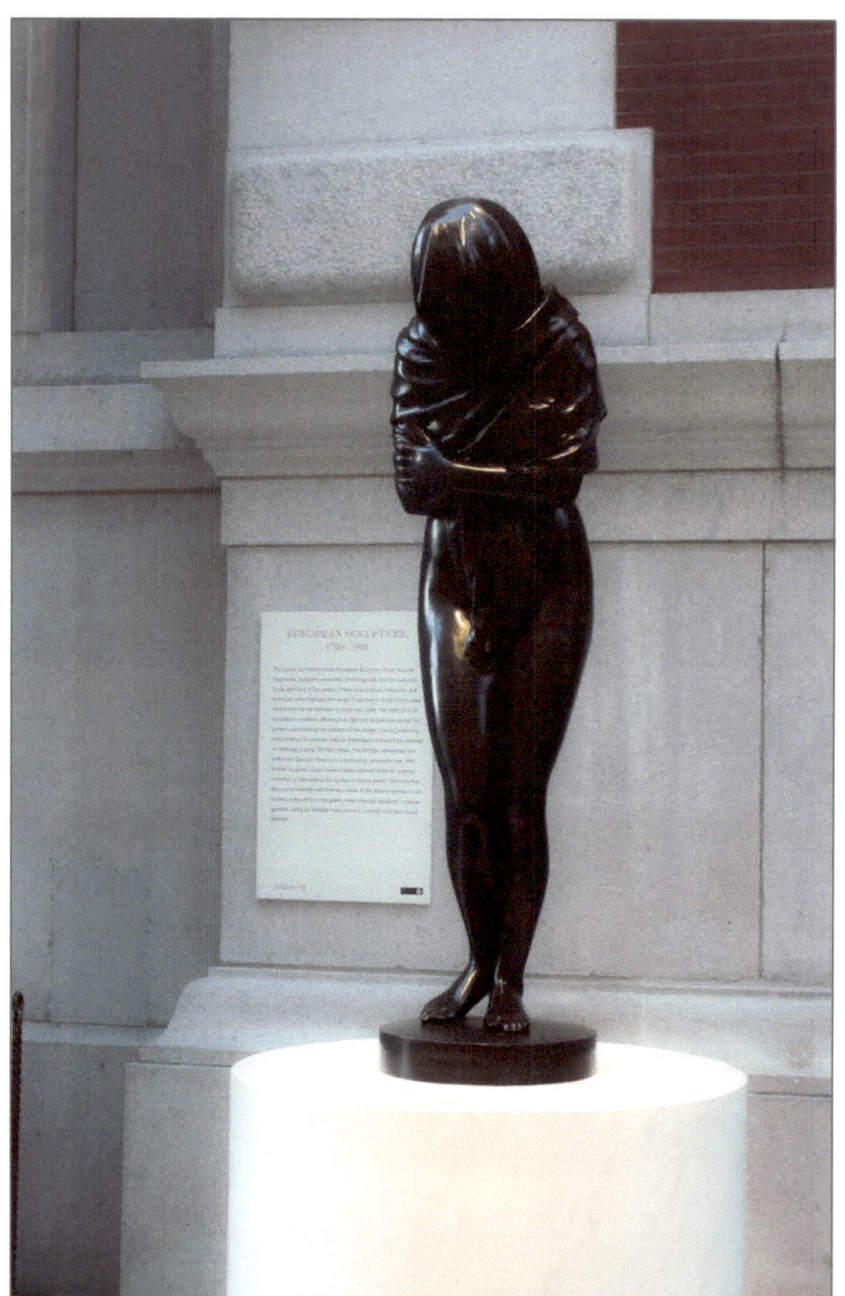

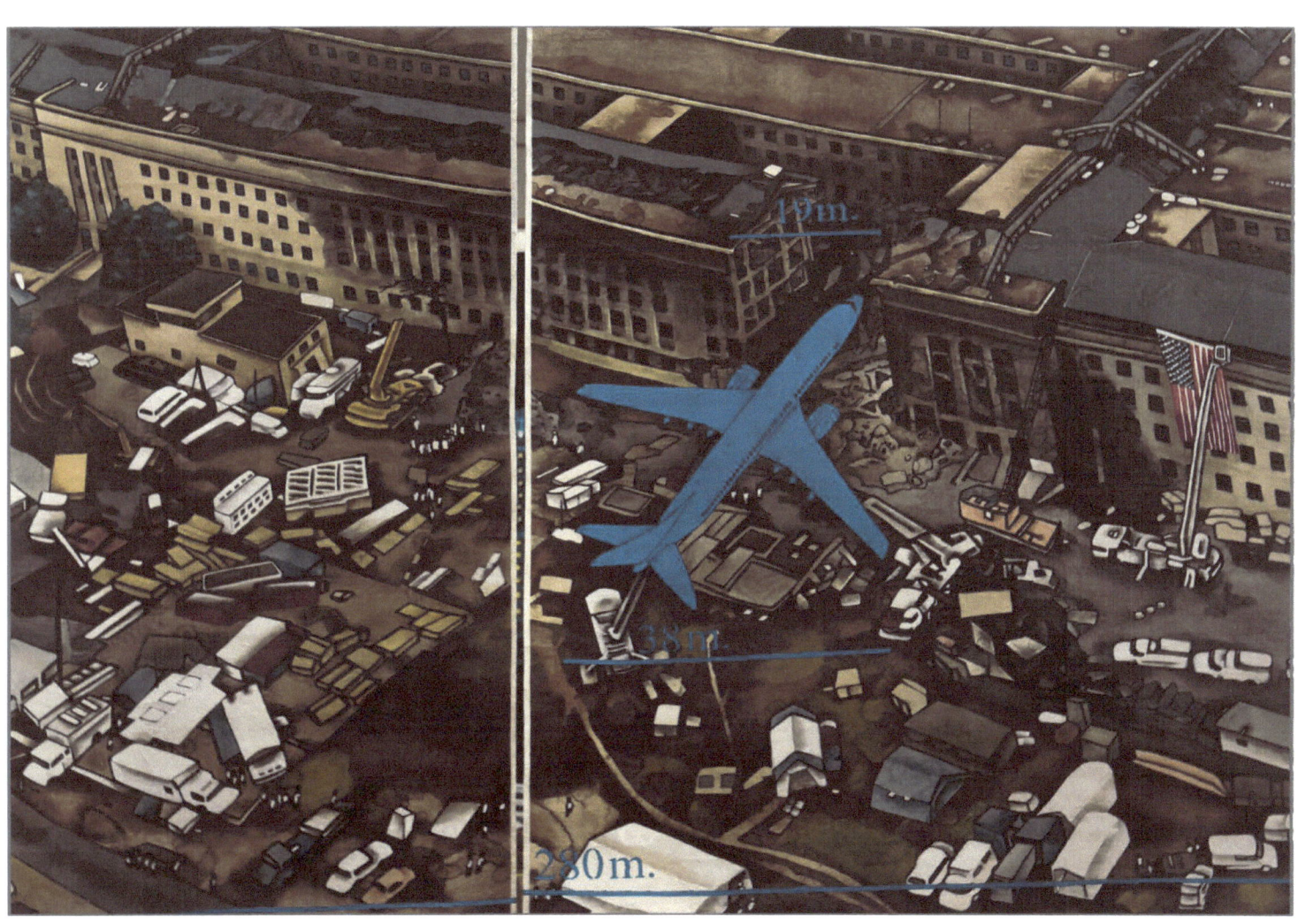

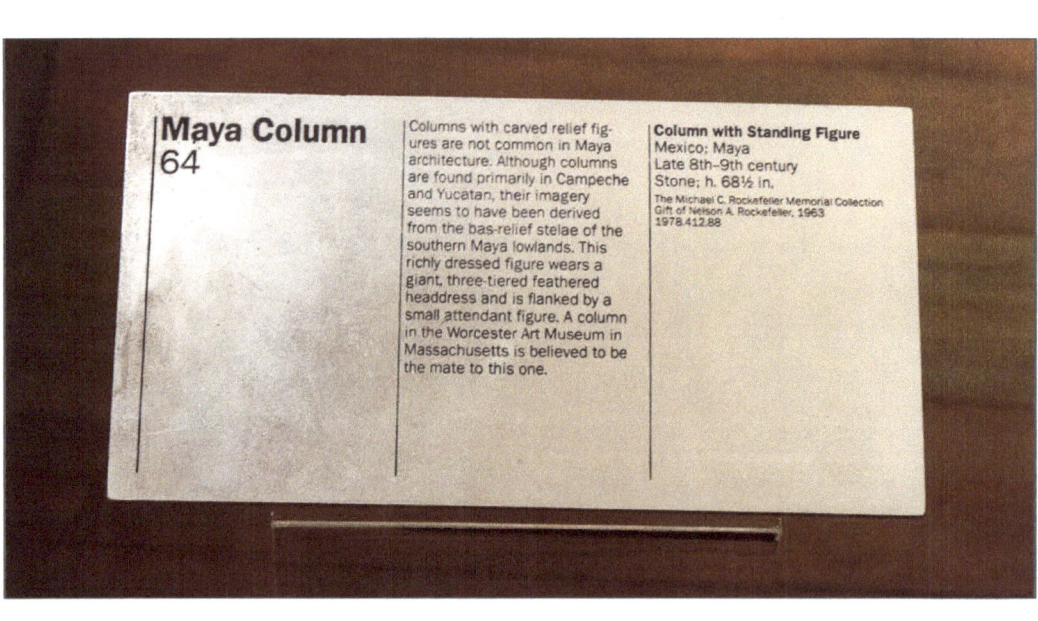

Maya Column
64

Columns with carved relief figures are not common in Maya architecture. Although columns are found primarily in Campeche and Yucatan, their imagery seems to have been derived from the bas-relief stelae of the southern Maya lowlands. This richly dressed figure wears a giant, three-tiered feathered headdress and is flanked by a small attendant figure. A column in the Worcester Art Museum in Massachusetts is believed to be the mate to this one.

Column with Standing Figure
Mexico; Maya
Late 8th–9th century
Stone; h. 68½ in.

The Michael C. Rockefeller Memorial Collection
Gift of Nelson A. Rockefeller, 1963
1978.412.88

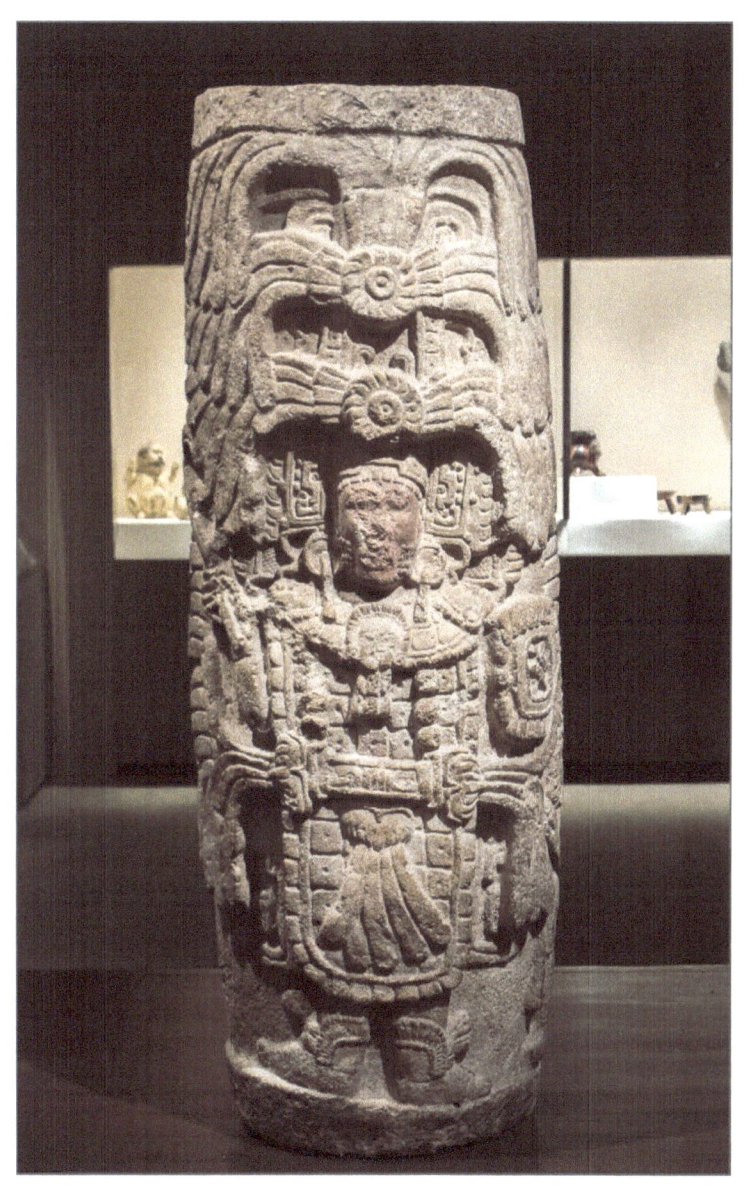

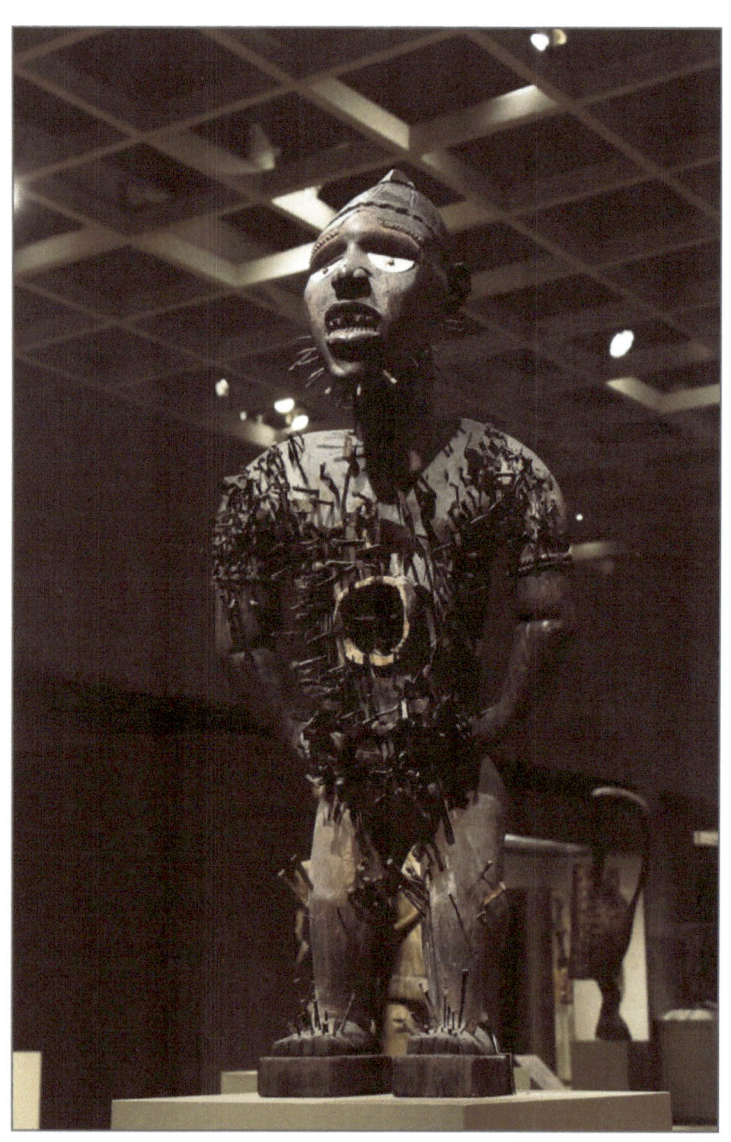

Kongo Power Figure

Nkisi N'Kondi: Mangaaka
Kongo Peoples, Chiloango River
Region; Democratic Republic of the
Congo or Angola
Second half of the 19th century
Wood, paint, metal, resin, ceramic

Purchase, Lila Acheson Wallace, Drs. Daniel and
Marian Malcolm, Laura G. and James J. Ross,
Jeffrey B. Soref, The Robert Wall Family, Dr. and
Mrs. Sidney G. Clyman, and Steven Kossak Gifts,
2008
2008.30

Central African power figures are
among the ubiquitous genres identified
with African art. Conceived to house
specific mystical forces, they were
collaborative creations of Kongo
sculptors and ritual specialists. This
example belongs to the most ambitious
class of that tradition, attributed to
the atelier of a master active along the
coast of Congo and Angola at the end
of the nineteenth century and identified
with Mangaaka, the preeminent force
of jurisprudence.

That power was represented
as a presiding authority and enforcing
lord or king. Its crowning element is
the distinctive mpu headdress worn by
chiefs or priests. The figure's posture
and gesture, leaning forward with
hands placed akimbo on the hips, is
the aggressive attitude of one who
challenges fearlessly. Traces of a
missing beard—a sign of seniority—
survive in the form of nails along
the contours of the chin. At some
undocumented time, the wood of
the front of the feet and supporting
rectangular blocks was subject to rot
or insect damage and has since been
restored with replacement parts. There
are also vestiges of an abdominal
cavity for medicinal matter that
originally attracted the figure's defining
force. The various metals embedded in
the figure's expansive torso attest to
its central role as witness and enforcer
of affairs critical to its community.
They document vows sealed, treaties
signed, and efforts to eradicate evil.
Ultimately, this work inspired reflection
on the consequences of transgressing
established codes of social conduct.

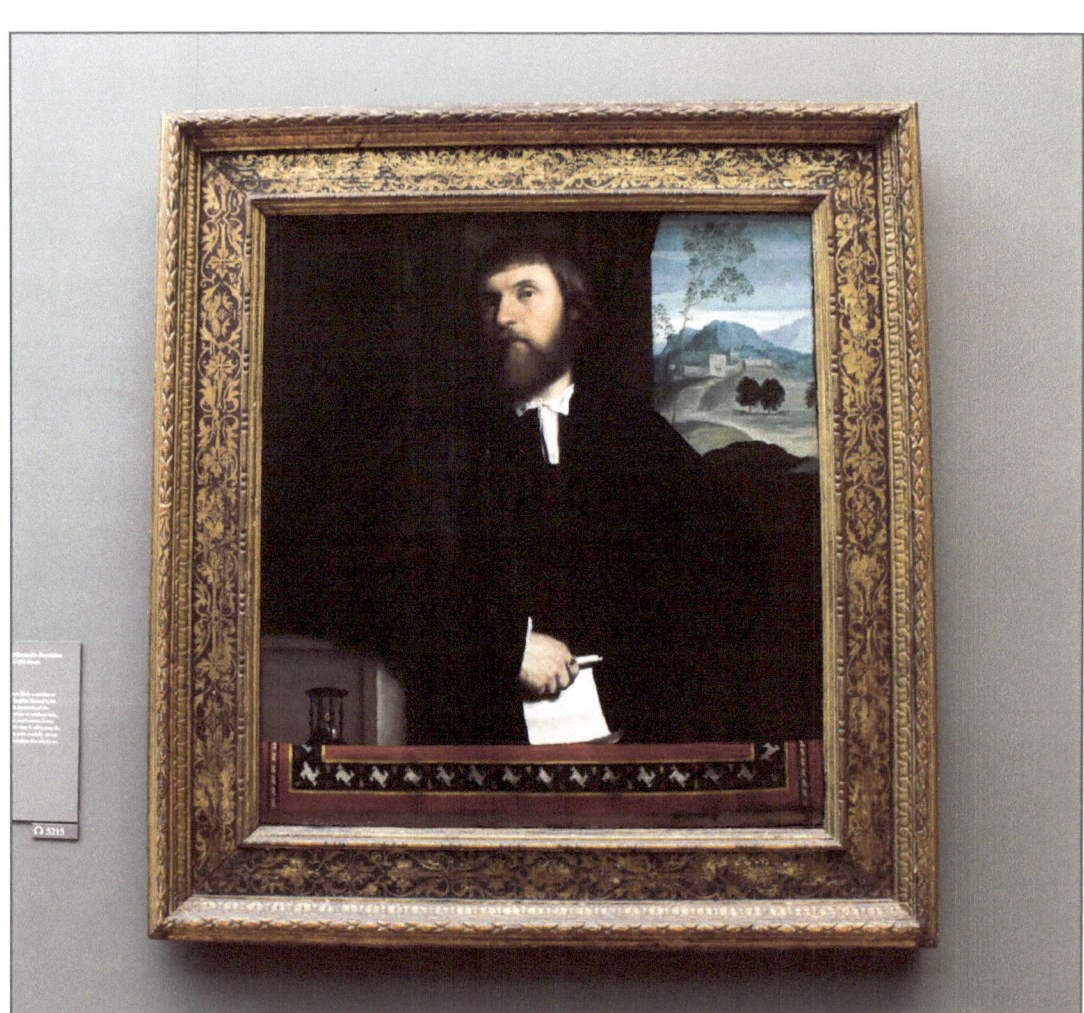

This unknown man is most likely a member of one of Brescia's wealthy families. Painted in the 1520s, it shows Moretto's awareness of the portraits being done elsewhere in northern Italy, principally those by Titian and Lorenzo Lotto. The artist suggests that the sitter is addressing the viewer, and surrounds him with carefully chosen accessories, such as the hourglass that alludes to the passage of time.

Rogers Fund, 1928
28.79

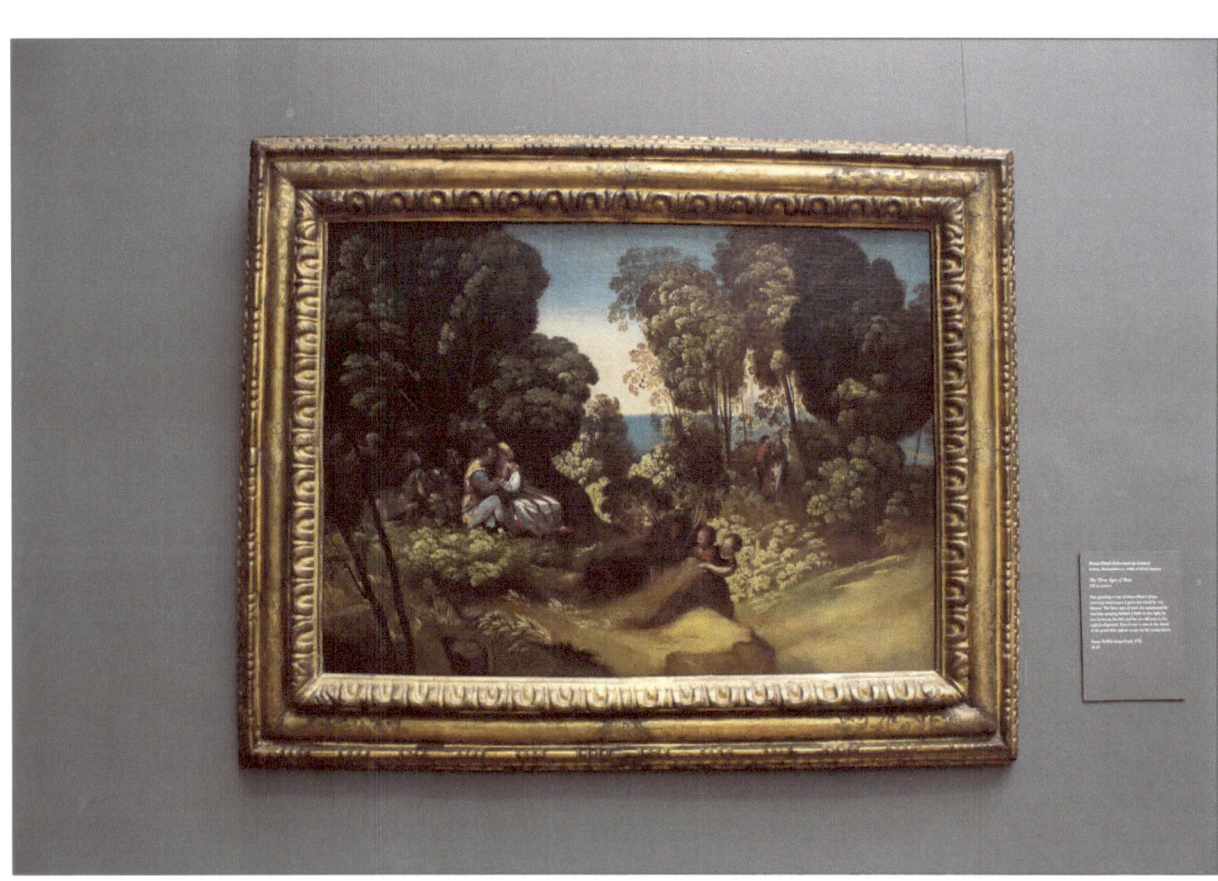

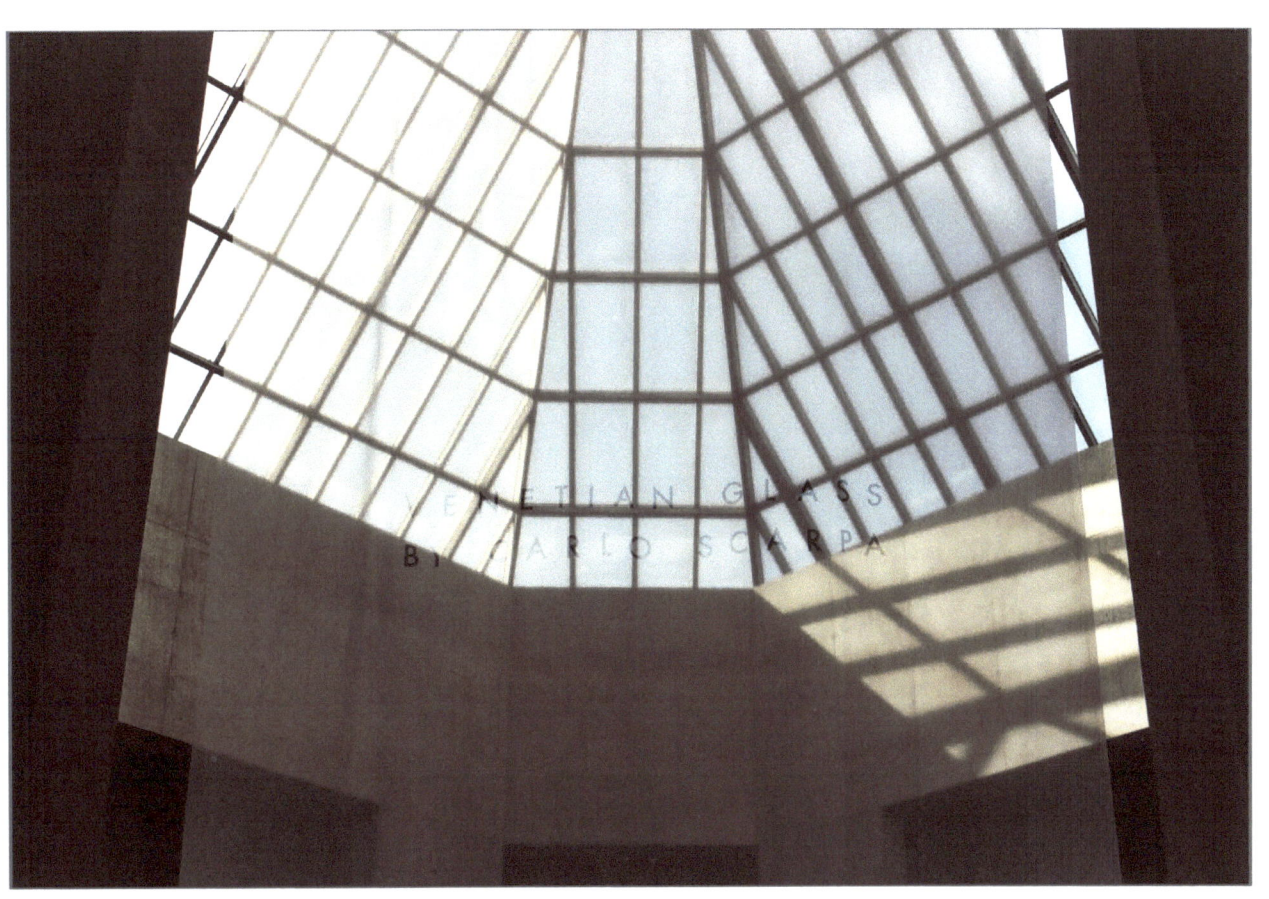

VENETIAN GLASS
BY CARLO SCARPA

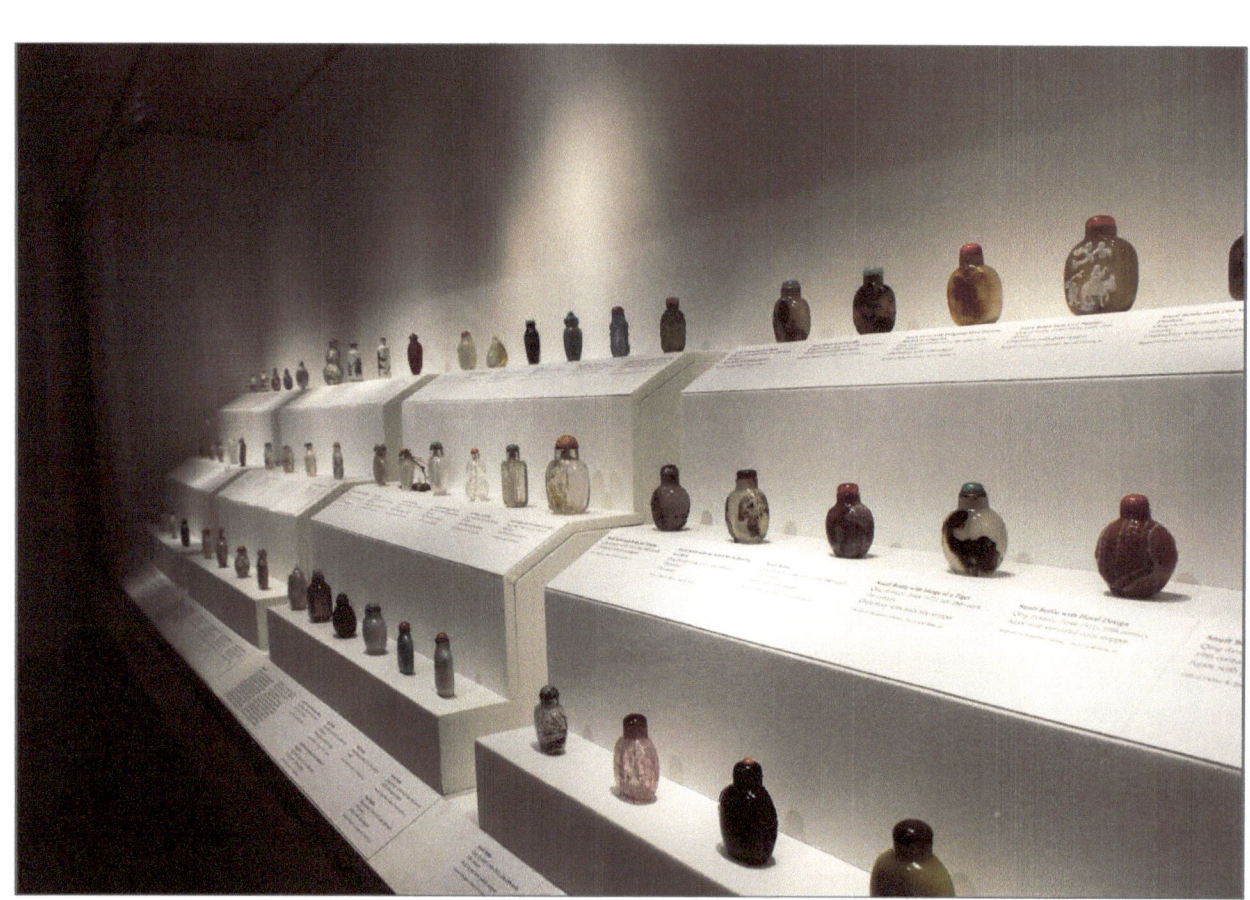

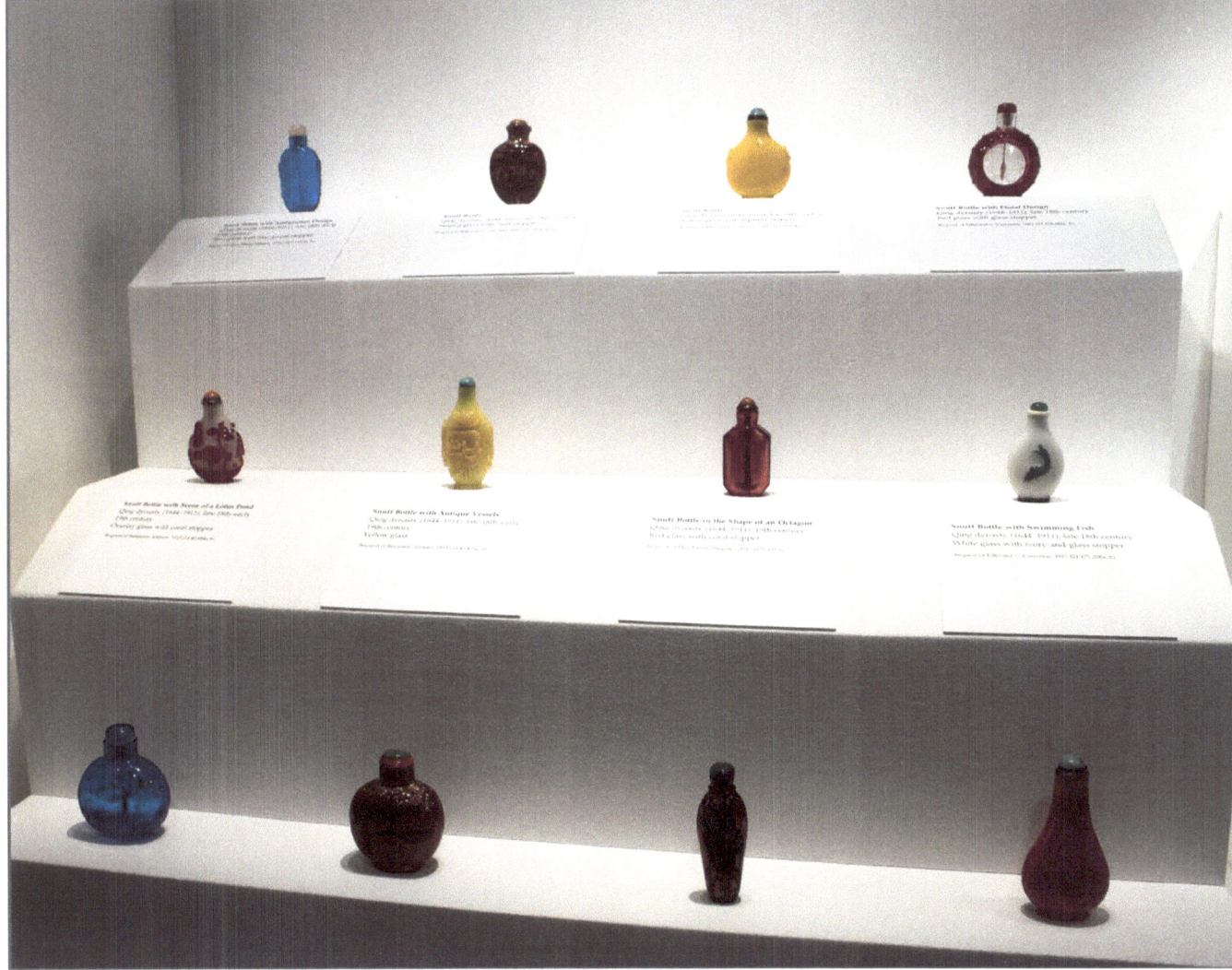

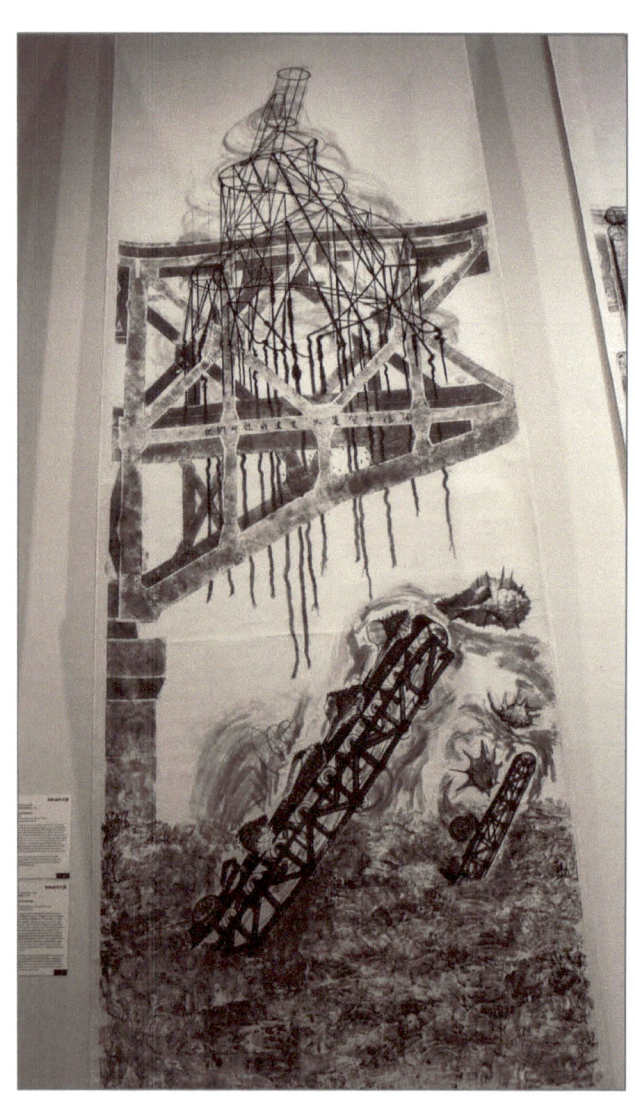

杨诘苍 会叫的风景
Yang Jiechang (b. 1956)

Crying Landscape
2002
Set of five triptychs; ink and color on paper
Private collection, New York

In *Crying Landscape,* Yang deploys the antique "blue-and-green" painting style on a grand scale to depict iconic man-made structures that connote political, industrial, or military power. The triptychs were first displayed at the 2003 Venice Biennale, where they were hung from the ceiling and accompanied by a soundtrack of Johan Strauss II's *The Blue Danube* waltz punctuated by the sound of the artist's screams. Arranged in the same order here, the sequence showcases the Houses of Parliament, an oil refinery, the great dam at the mouth of the Yangzi Gorges, the Pentagon under terrorist attack, and a Las Vegas simulacrum of New York. Yang here undermines the promise of stability, prosperity, and security symbolized by these iconic buildings.

The large scale, intense colors, and representational style of *Crying Landscape* find parallels in the Buddhist mural on view in this gallery. As a student, Yang made close copies of similar fourteenth-century murals.

 301

黄岩　中国山水纹身

Huang Yan (b. 1966)

Chinese Landscape Tattoo No. 2 and No. 4
1999
Two chromogenic prints
Private collection, New York

In his 1999 photographic series *Chinese Landscape Tattoo*, Huang covers his torso and arms with traditional landscape scenes, presenting his "reincarnation" of literati-style painting. The composition, modeled in ink and colors on a white ground by Huang's wife, the artist Zhang Tiemei (b. 1968), follows the natural form of Huang's body. In the photos, the artist's face is cropped away and Huang's anonymous torso becomes an emblem of the Chinese everyman who cannot be separated from his cultural heritage, which, like his racial identity, is as indelible as a tattoo.

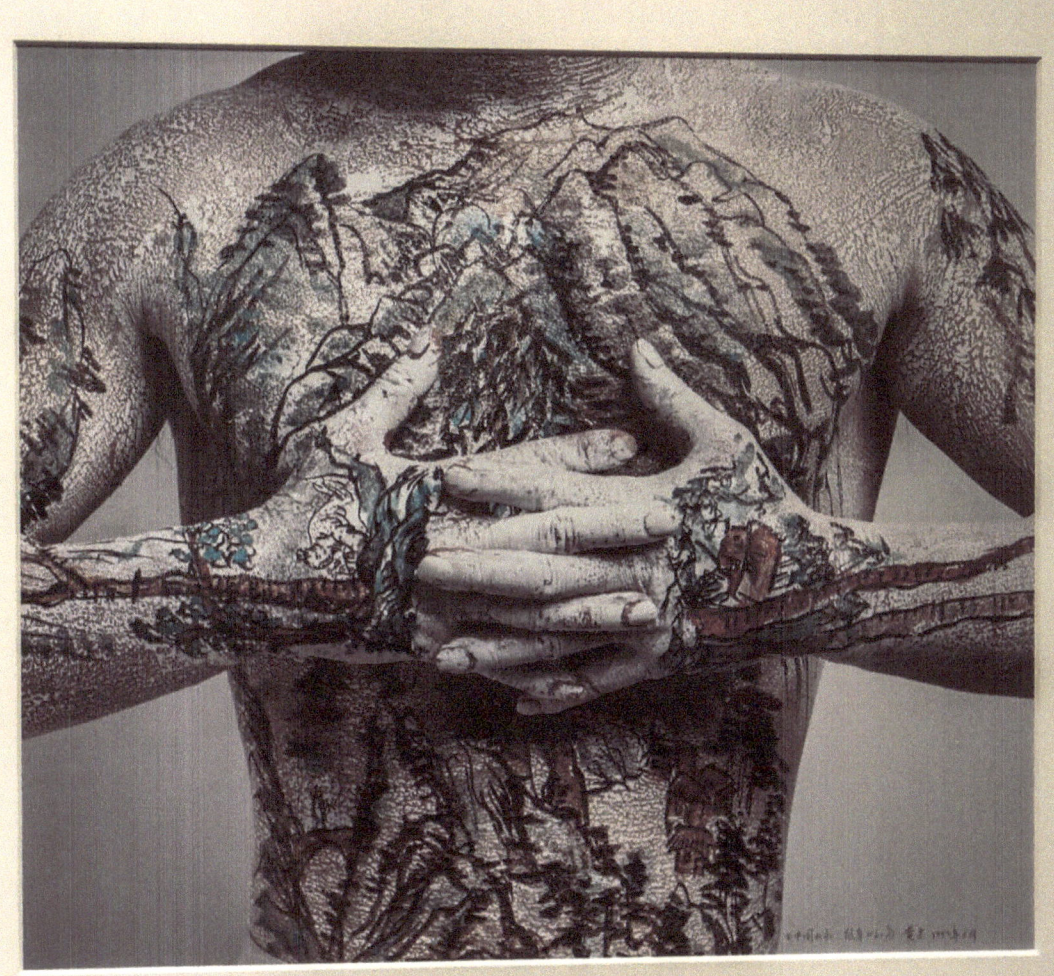

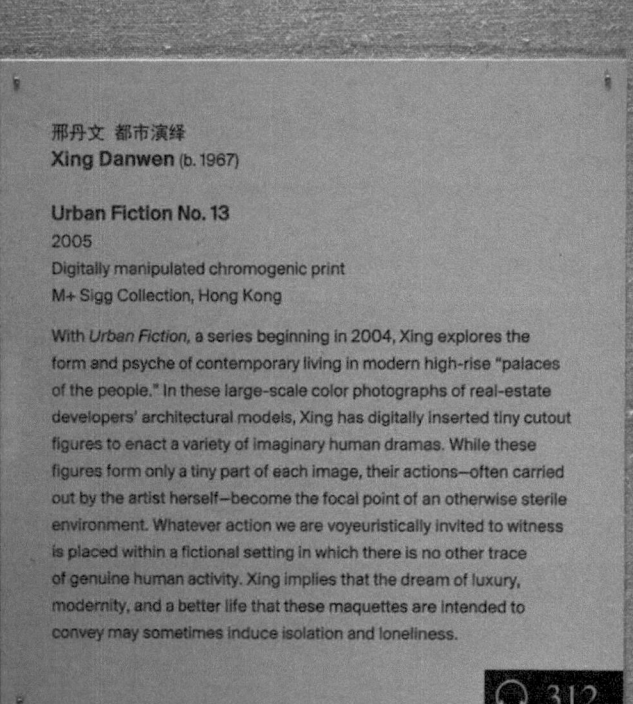

邢丹文　都市演绎
Xing Danwen (b. 1967)

Urban Fiction No. 13
2005
Digitally manipulated chromogenic print
M+ Sigg Collection, Hong Kong

With *Urban Fiction*, a series beginning in 2004, Xing explores the
form and psyche of contemporary living in modern high-rise "palaces
of the people." In these large-scale color photographs of real-estate
developers' architectural models, Xing has digitally inserted tiny cutout
figures to enact a variety of imaginary human dramas. While these
figures form only a tiny part of each image, their actions—often carried
out by the artist herself—become the focal point of an otherwise sterile
environment. Whatever action we are voyeuristically invited to witness
is placed within a fictional setting in which there is no other trace
of genuine human activity. Xing implies that the dream of luxury,
modernity, and a better life that these maquettes are intended to
convey may sometimes induce isolation and loneliness.

🎧 312

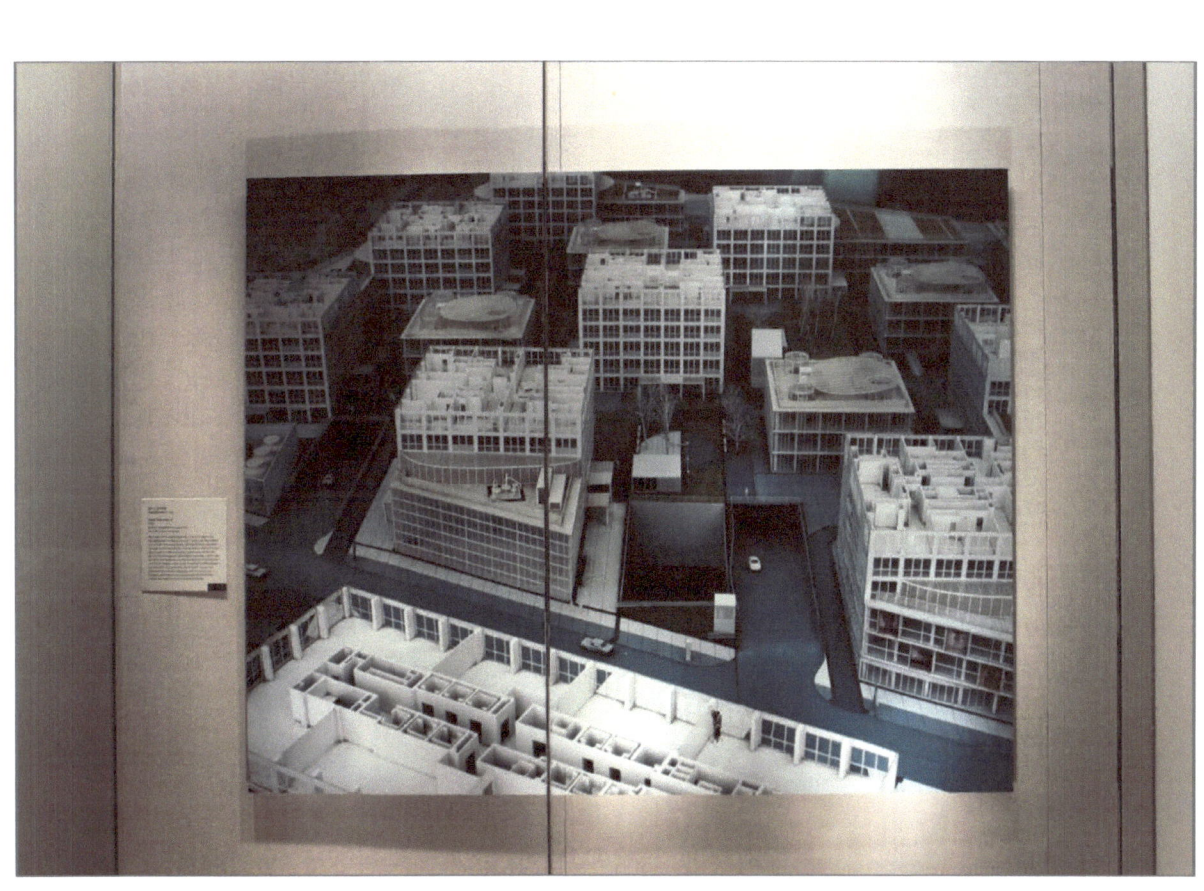

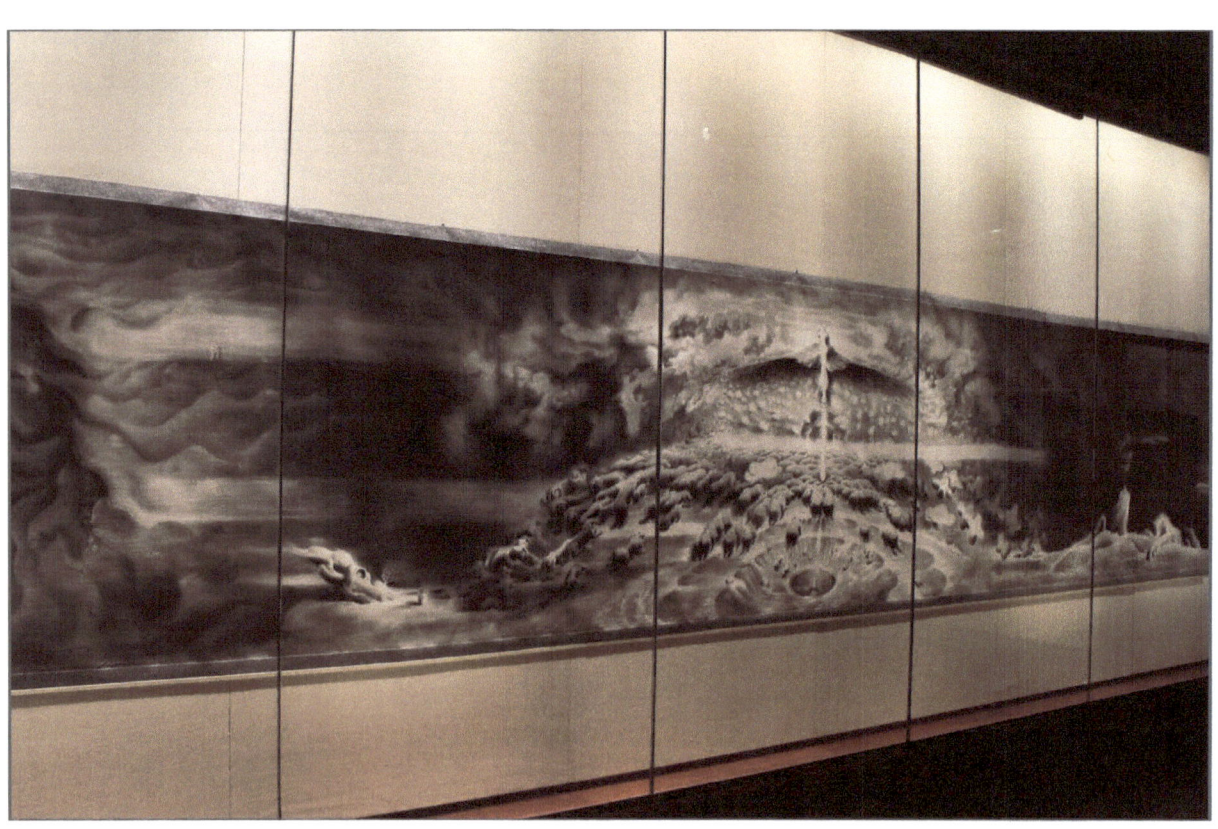

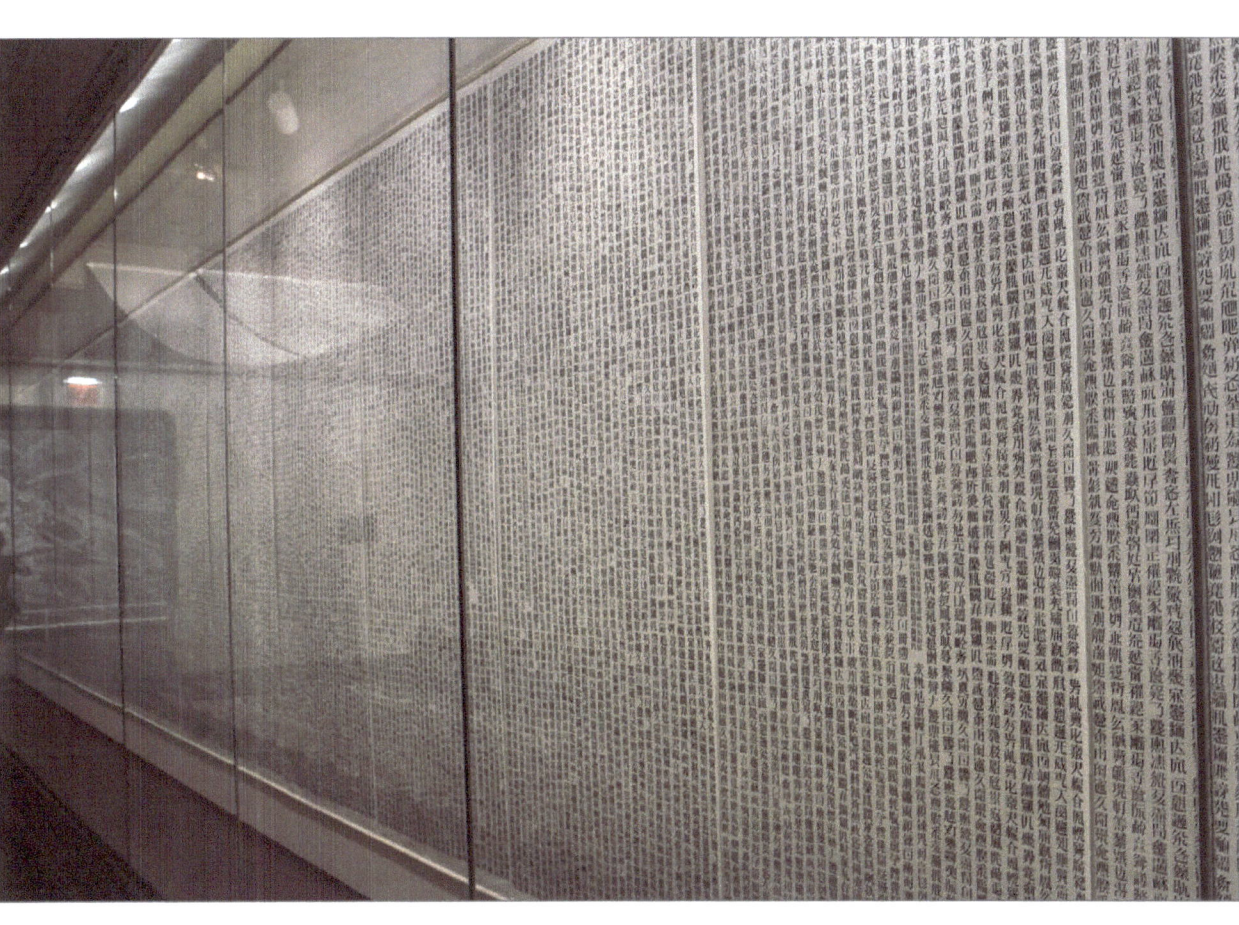

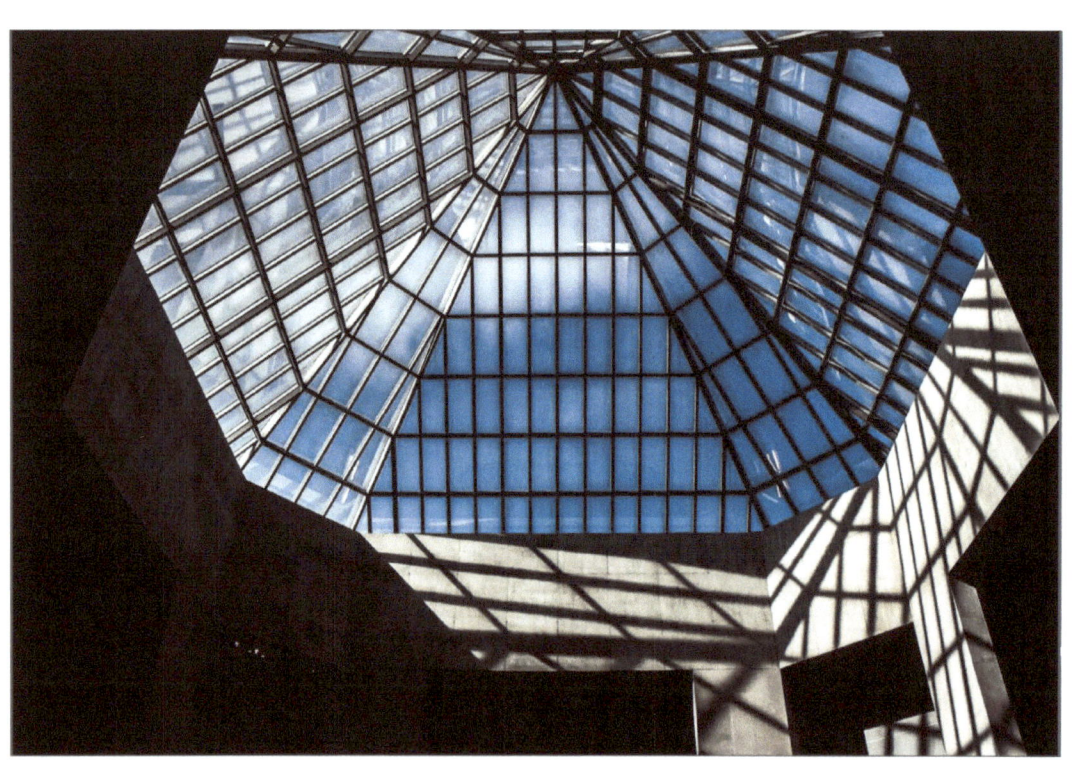

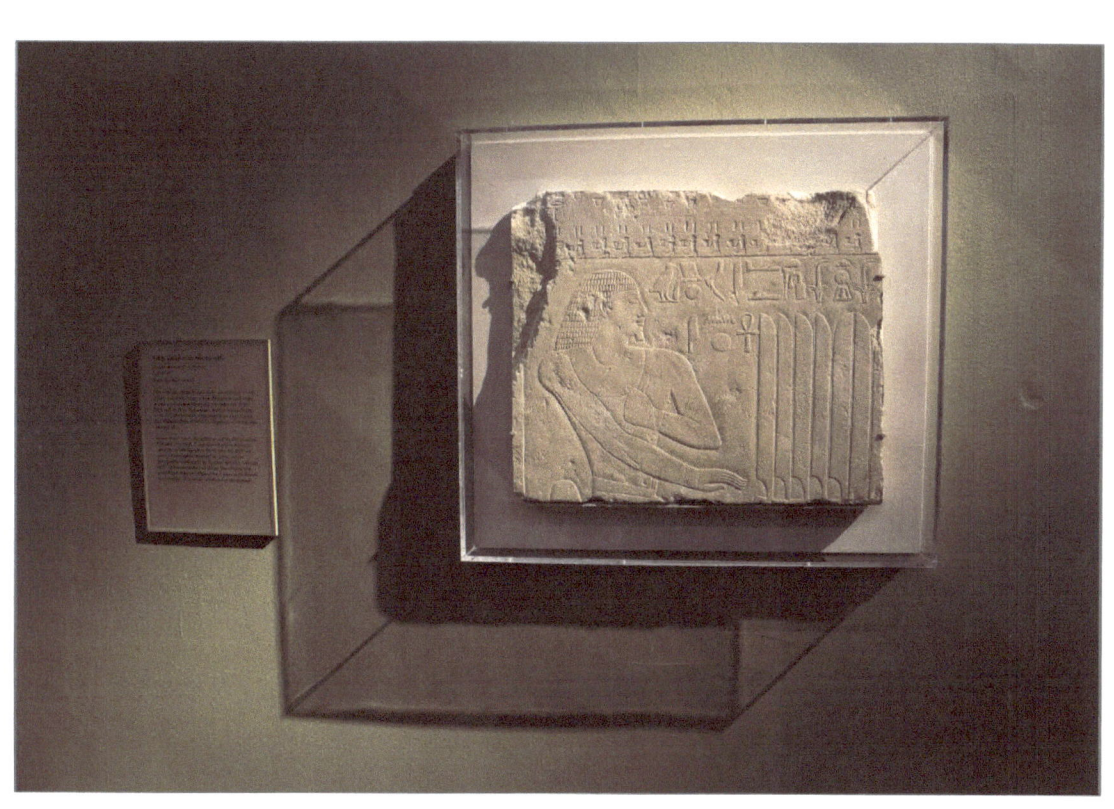

史国瑞 上海
Shi Guorui (b. 1964)

Shanghai, China, 15–16 October 2004
2004
Unique camera obscura gelatin silver print
M+ Sigg Collection, Hong Kong

This eerie image of contemporary Shanghai was created using a
camera obscura, an ancient technology for projecting images that
Shi has adopted for his artistic practice. To create a print with this
method, light is projected through a small hole onto a sheet of
photographic paper for hours while the image is exposed. Because
the exposure takes such a long time, the frenetic movement of
people and vehicles that animates the city does not register in the
resulting print. Instead, we are presented with one of the world's
largest and most dynamic cities rendered as a silent vista—a new
landscape for the twenty-first century.

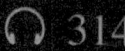 314

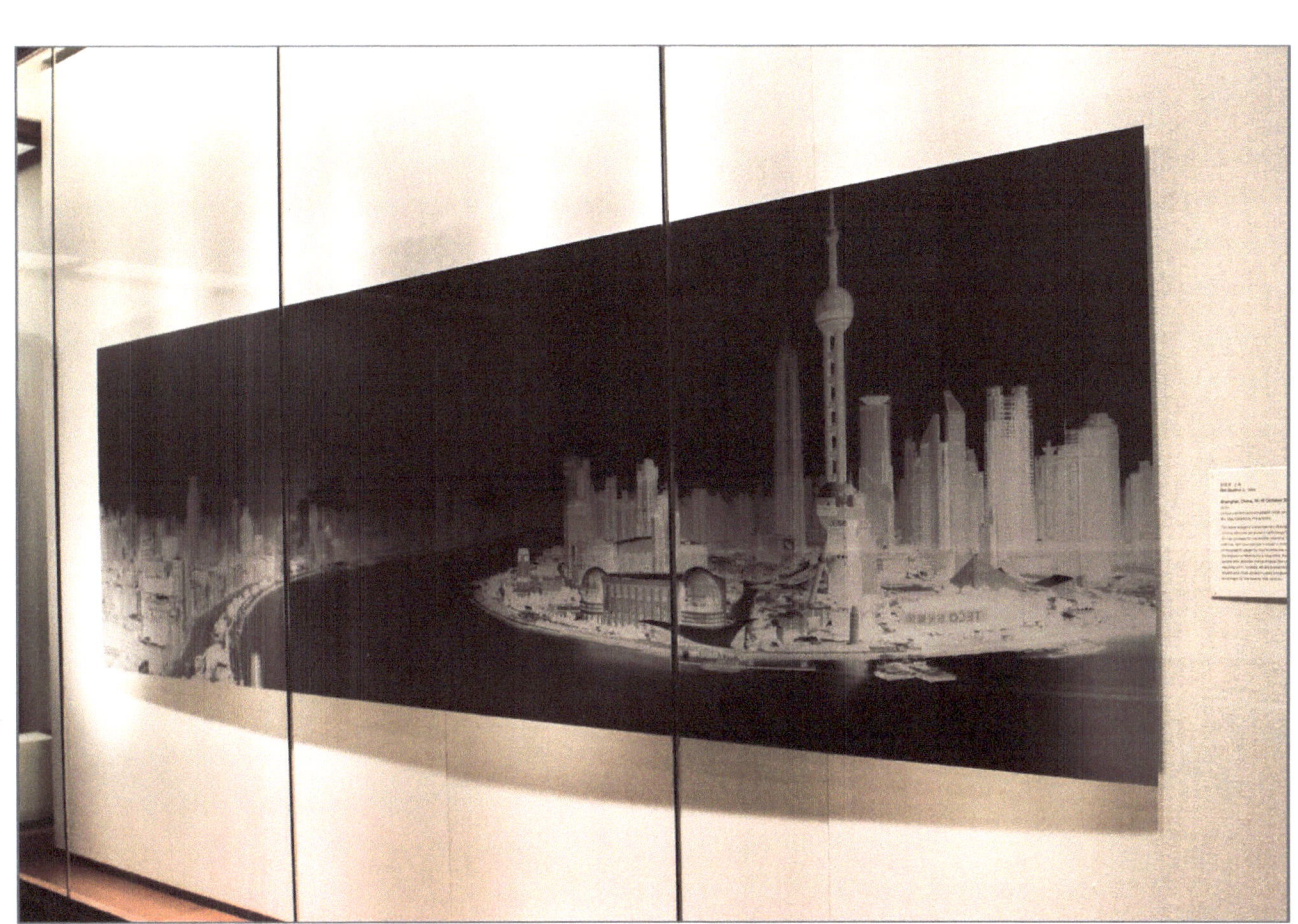

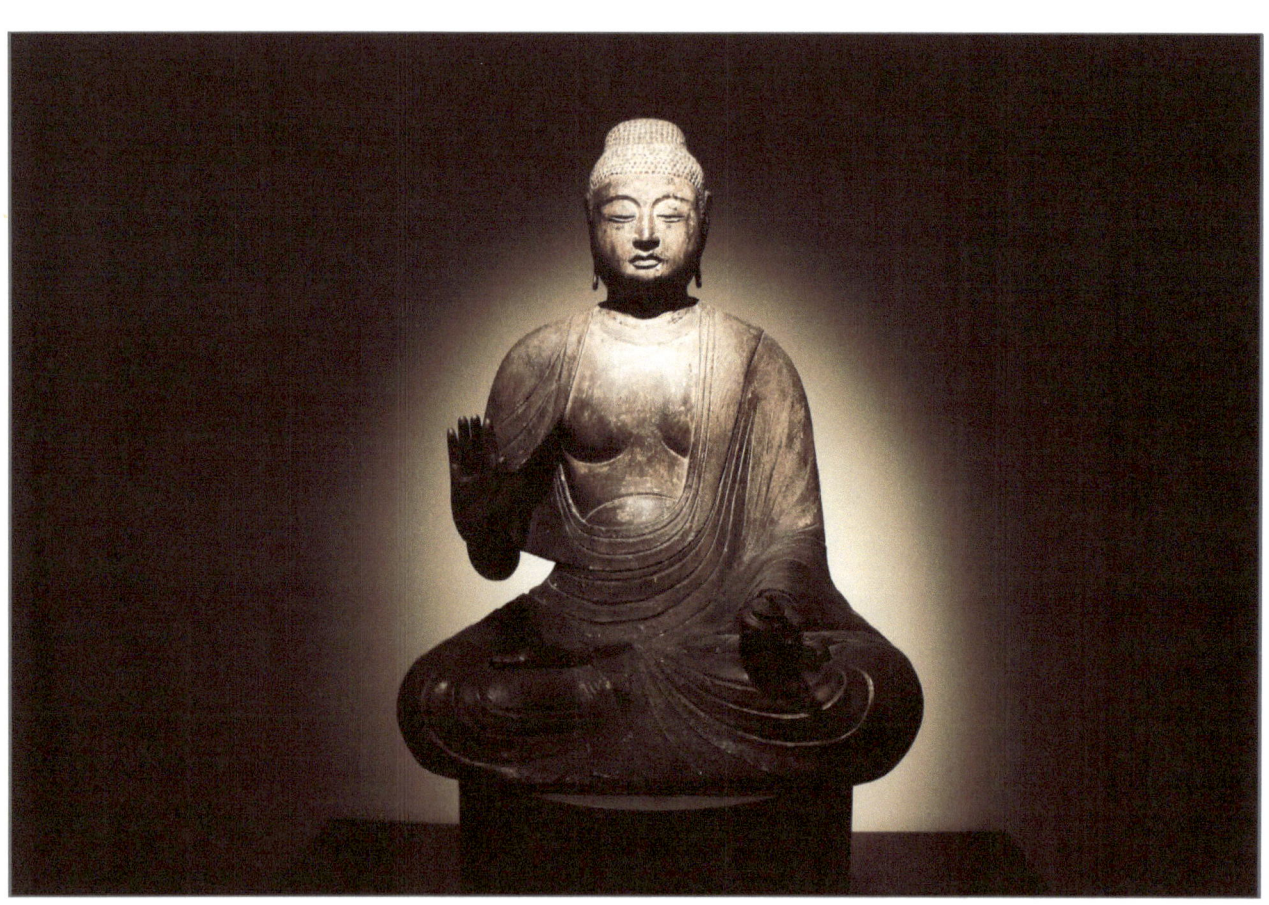

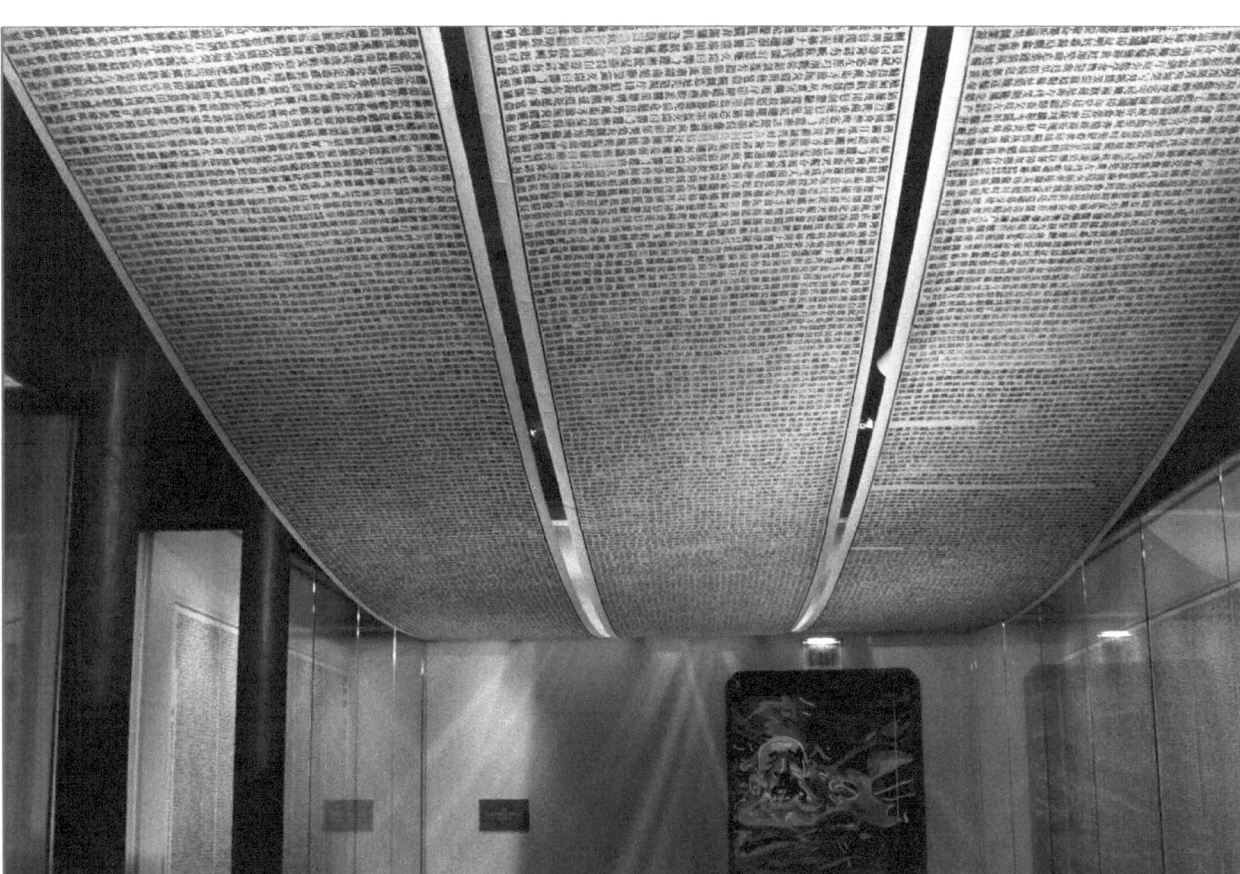

深見陶治作 「屹」

Fukami Sueharu (born 1947)
"Upright" (Kitsu)
Heisei period (1989–present), 2012
Pale-blue glazed porcelain; granite base

Purchase, Anonymous Gift, 2013 (2013.168a, b)

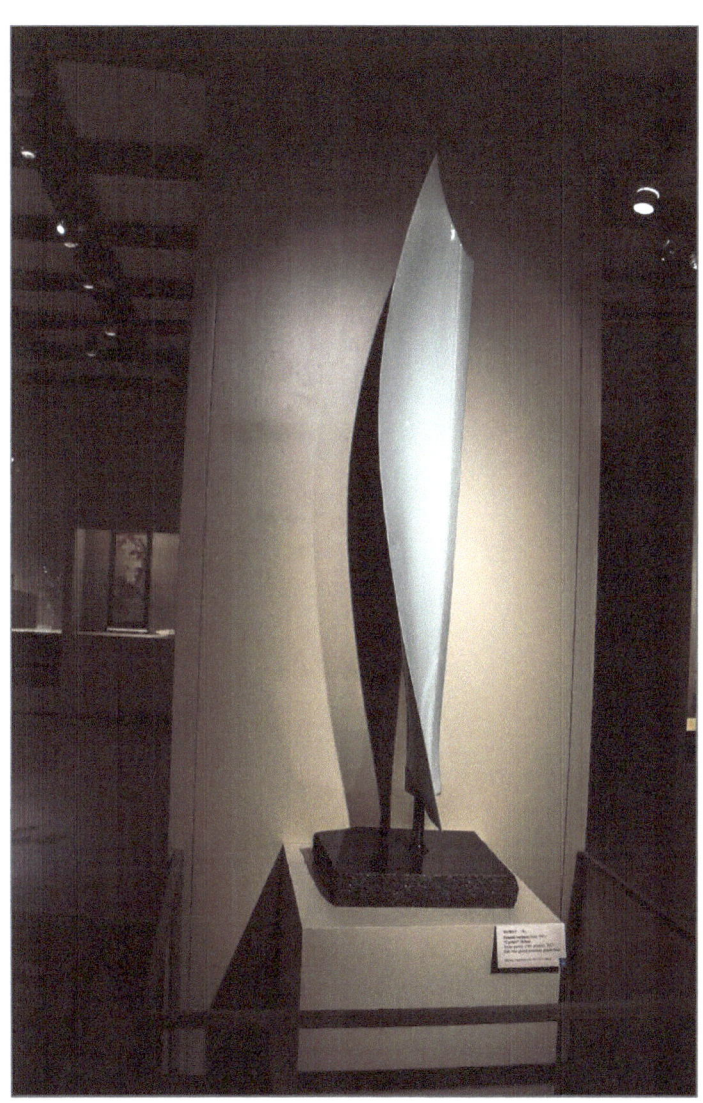

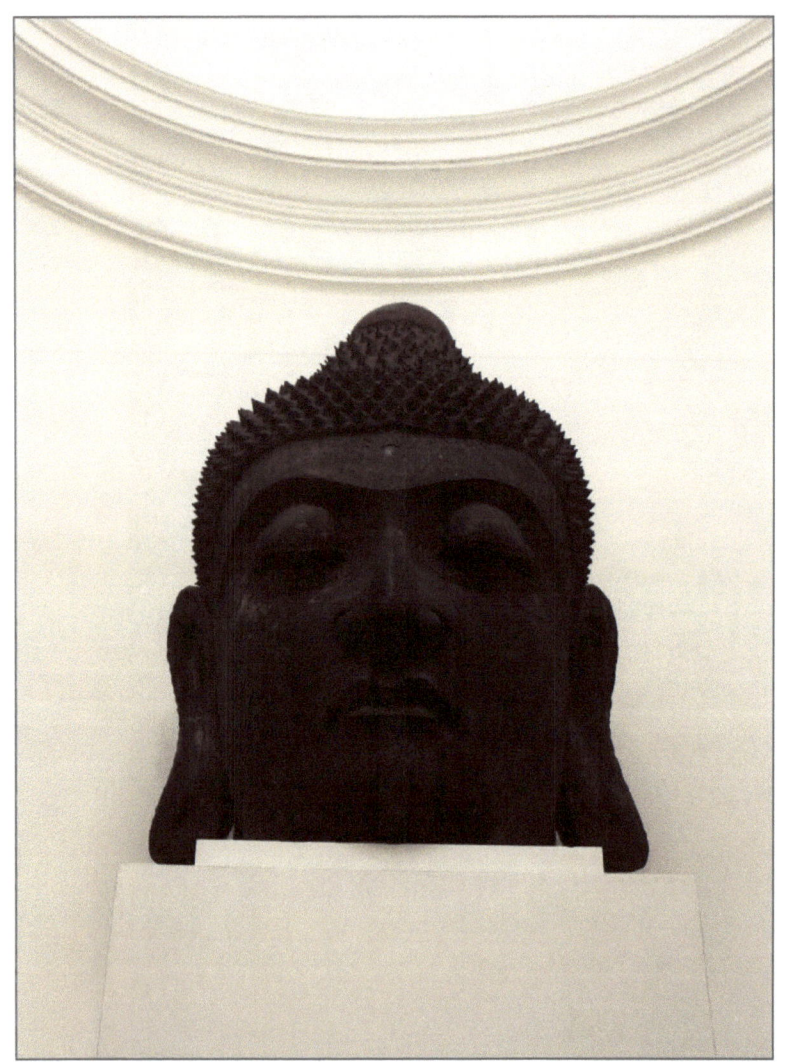

Head of a Buddha
Ming dynasty (1368–1644), ca. 1500
Shanxi Province
Cast iron

Fletcher Fund, 1961
61.94

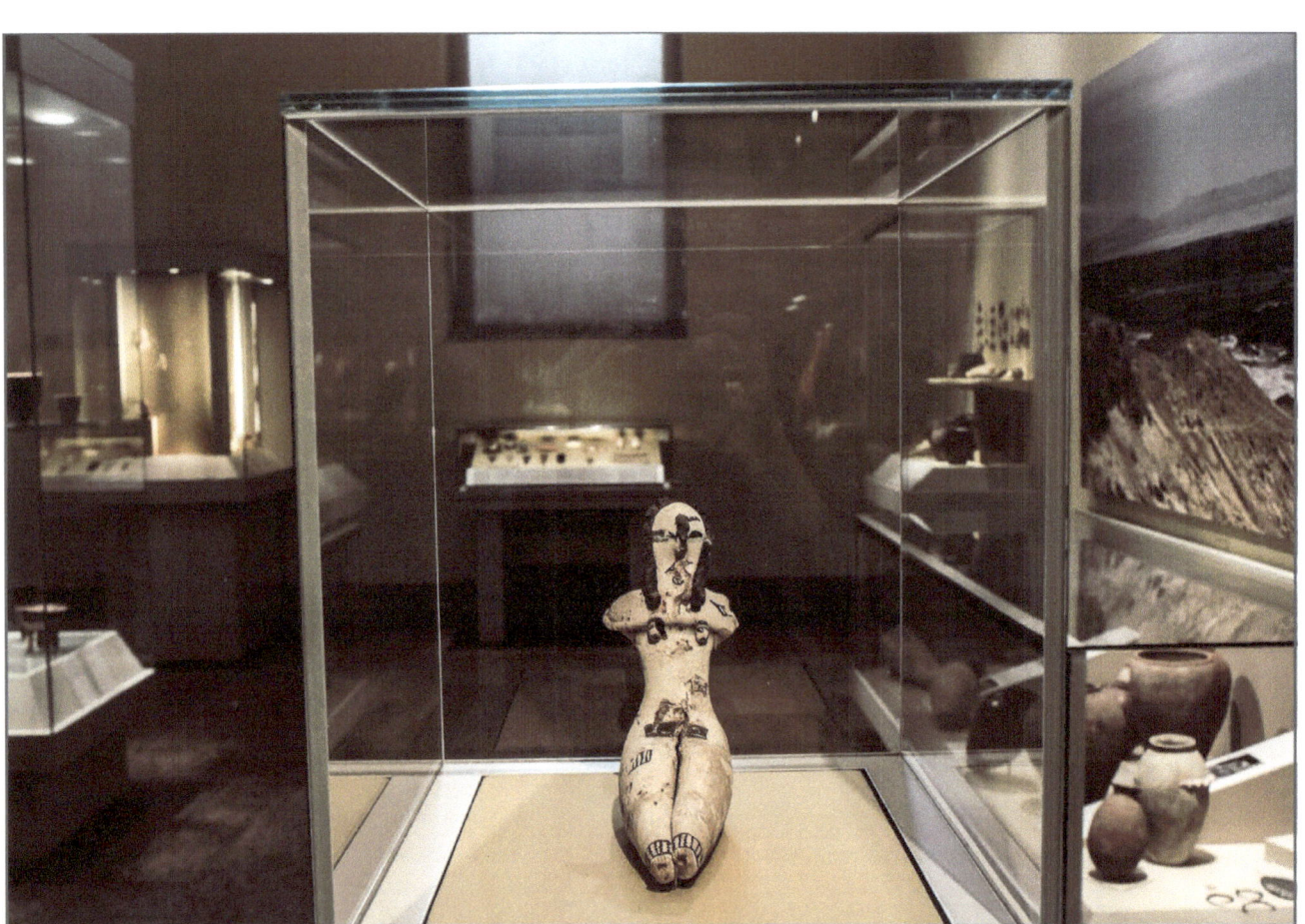

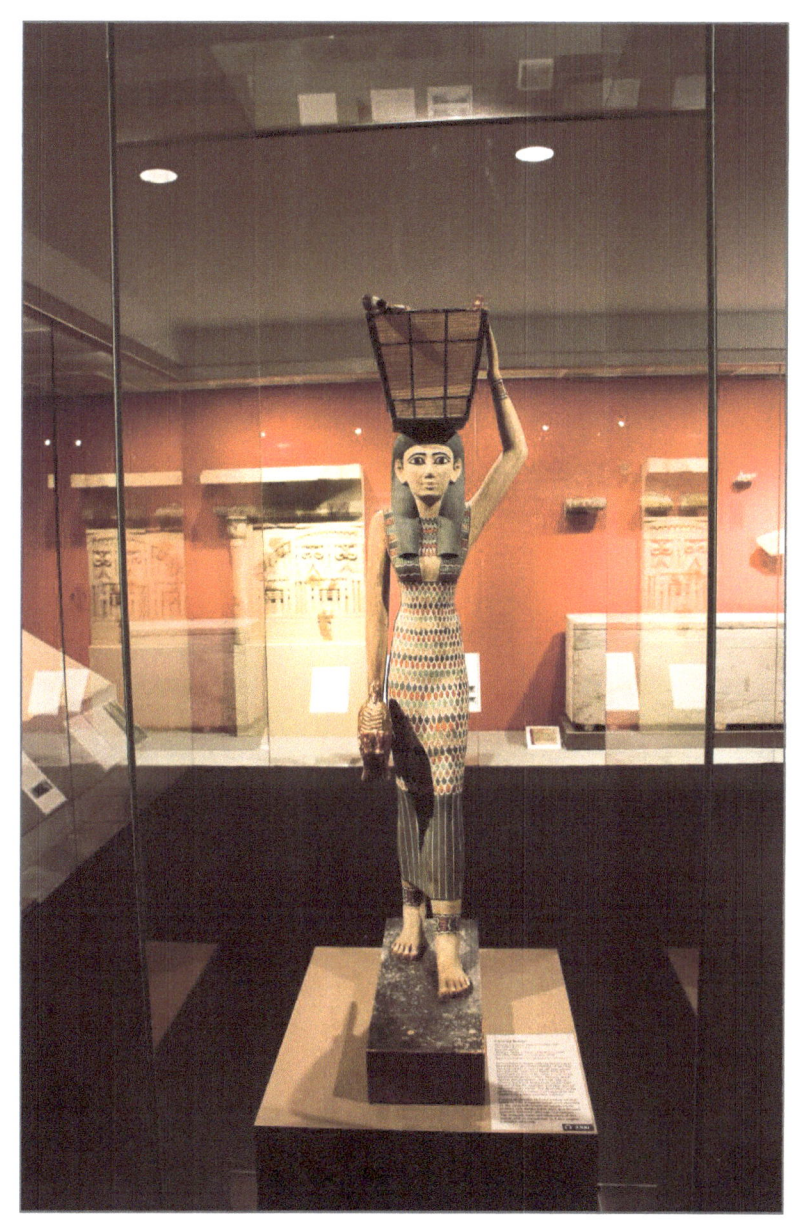

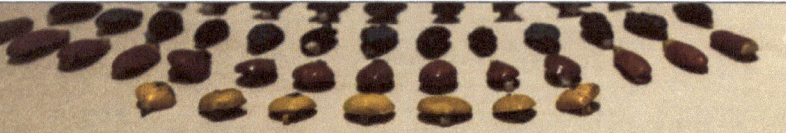

Signet Ring
Dynasty 18, reign of Tutankhamun, ca. 1336–1327 B.C.
Gold

Gift of Edward S. Harkness, 1922 (22.9.3)

This horizontal signet ring shows signs of wear from
frequent use as a seal. It is inscribed down the center with
Tutankhamun's prenomen, Neb-kheperu-re; on either side
the king is referred to as "beloved of Amun, lord of eternity."

Signet Ring
Dynasty 18, reign of Akhenaten, ca. 1353–1336 B.C.
Gold
From Amarna

Purchase, Edward S. Harkness Gift, 1926 (26.7.767)

The hieroglyphs on this ring may be read as an ideo-
gram. The two seated figures are probably Akhenaten (left)
and Nefertiti (right) as the deities Shu (air) and Tefnut
(moisture). They were father and mother of the earth
and sky, which are symbolically represented by the earth
hieroglyph (below) and by the sun disk flanked by two
sacred cobras (above).

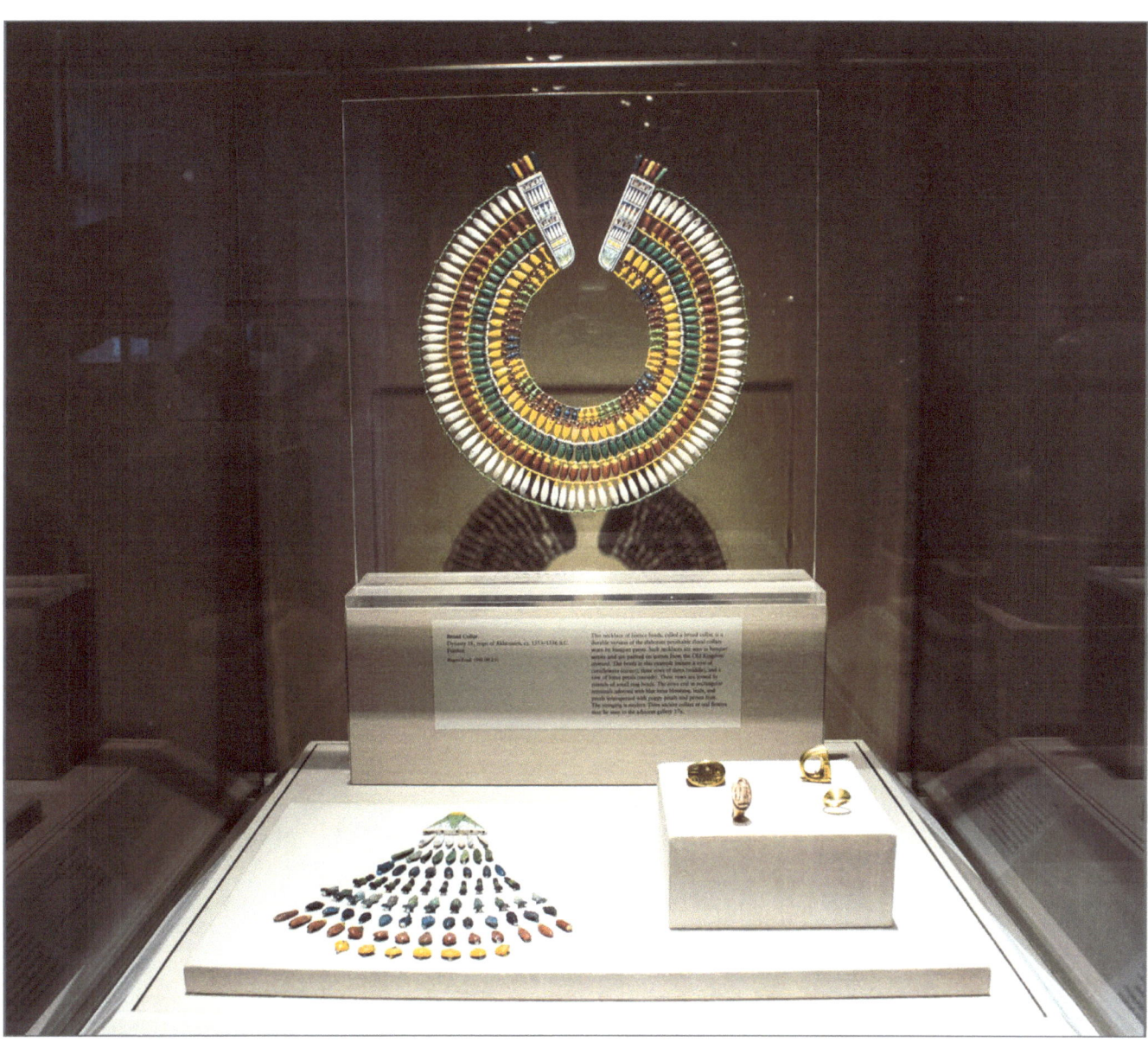

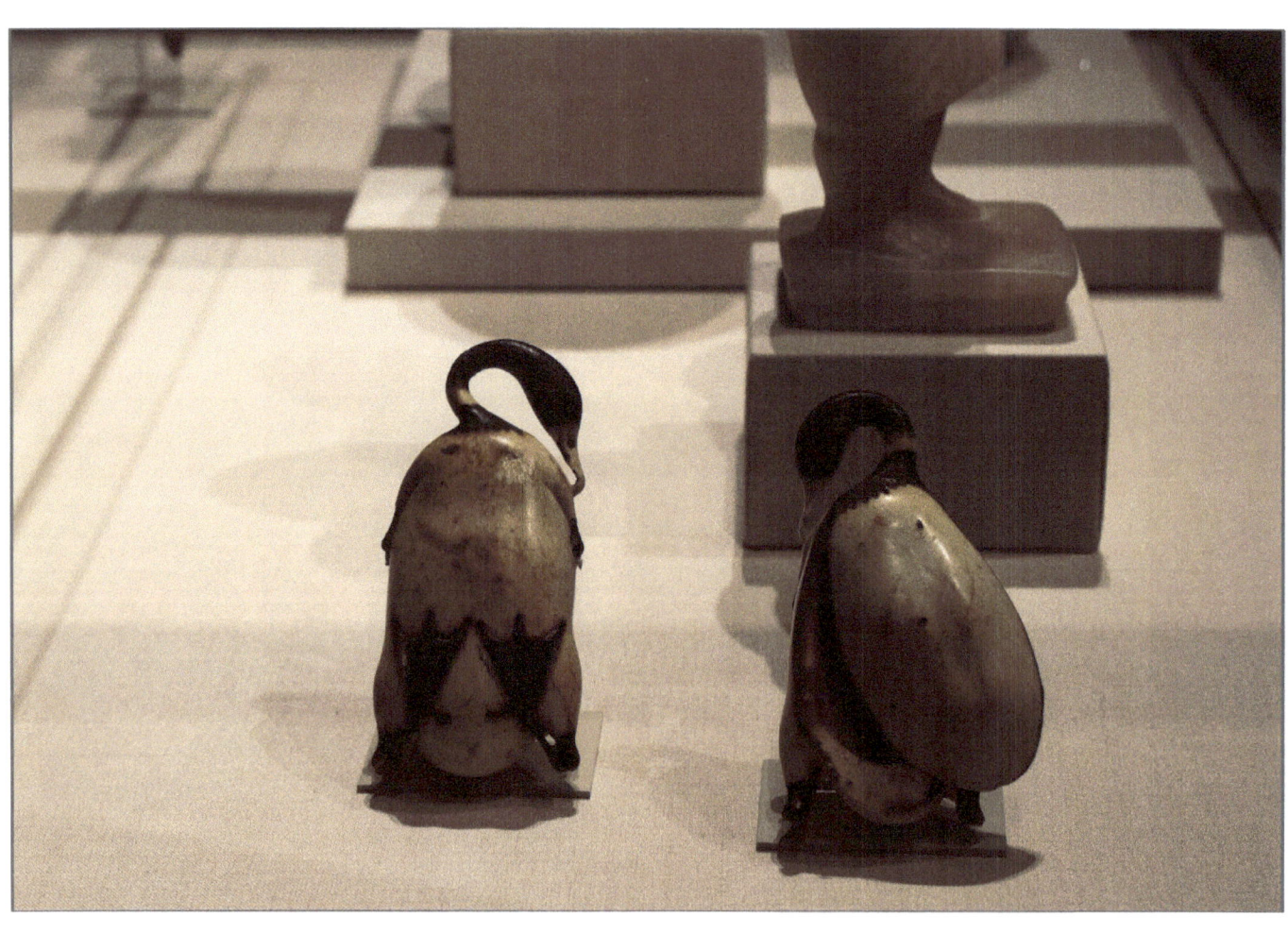

Cosmetic Boxes in the Shape of Trussed Ducks

Dynasty 18, reigns of Akhenaten–Tutankhamun,
ca. 1353–1327 B.C.
Ivory

Rogers Fund, 1940 (40.2.2, .3)

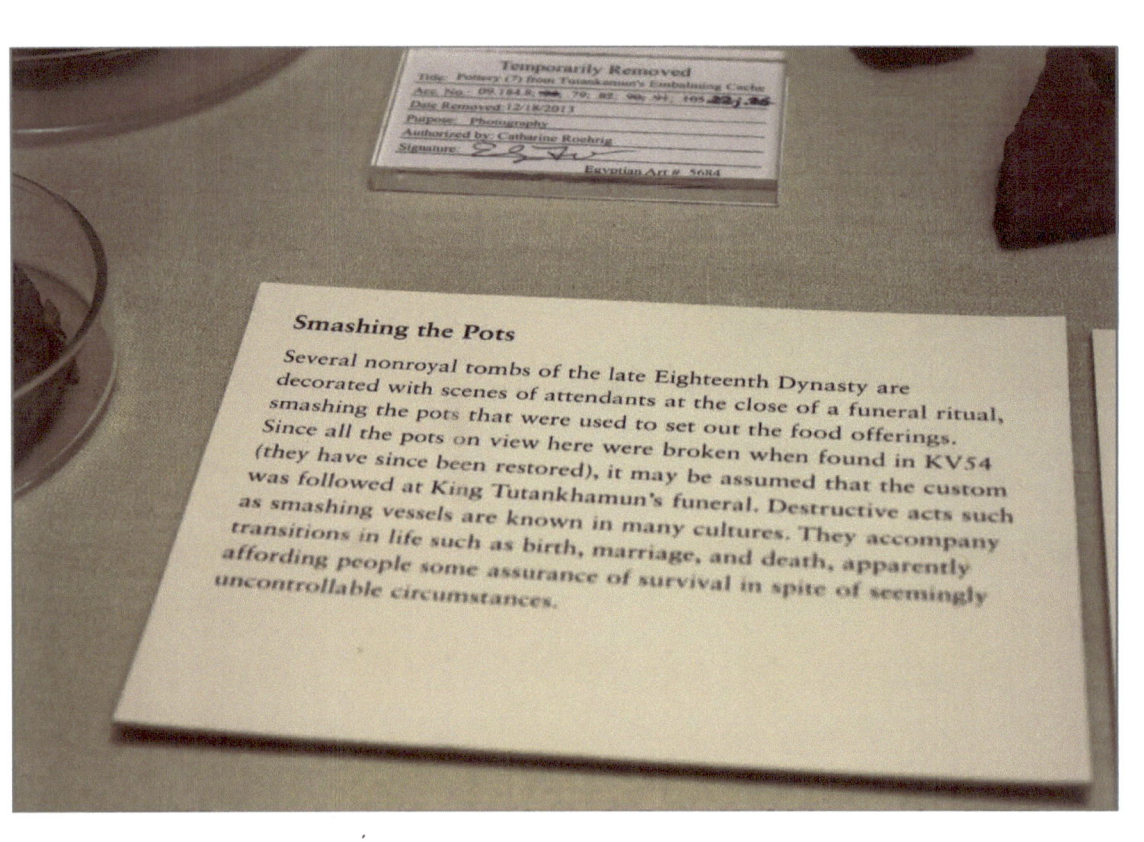

Smashing the Pots

Several nonroyal tombs of the late Eighteenth Dynasty are decorated with scenes of attendants at the close of a funeral ritual, smashing the pots that were used to set out the food offerings. Since all the pots on view here were broken when found in KV54 (they have since been restored), it may be assumed that the custom was followed at King Tutankhamun's funeral. Destructive acts such as smashing vessels are known in many cultures. They accompany transitions in life such as birth, marriage, and death, apparently affording people some assurance of survival in spite of seemingly uncontrollable circumstances.

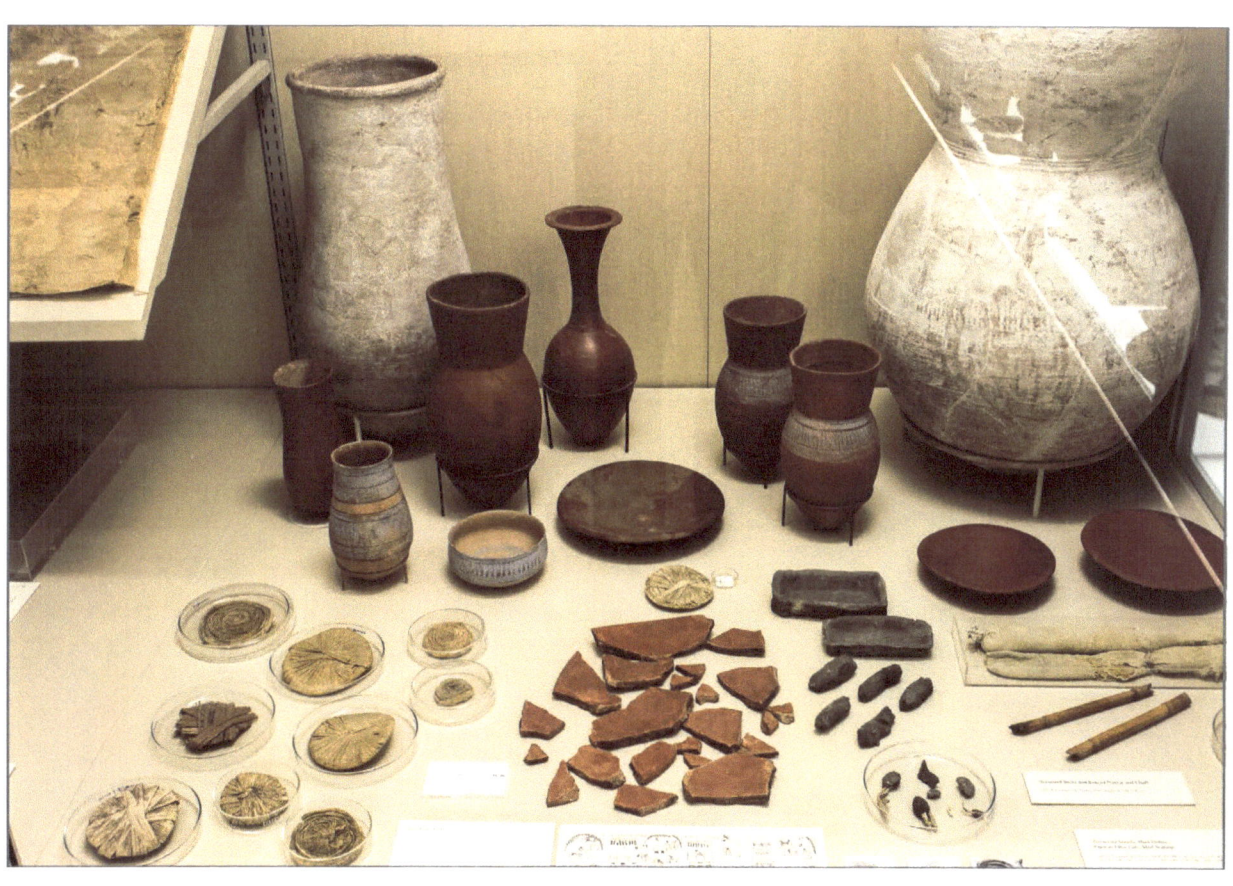

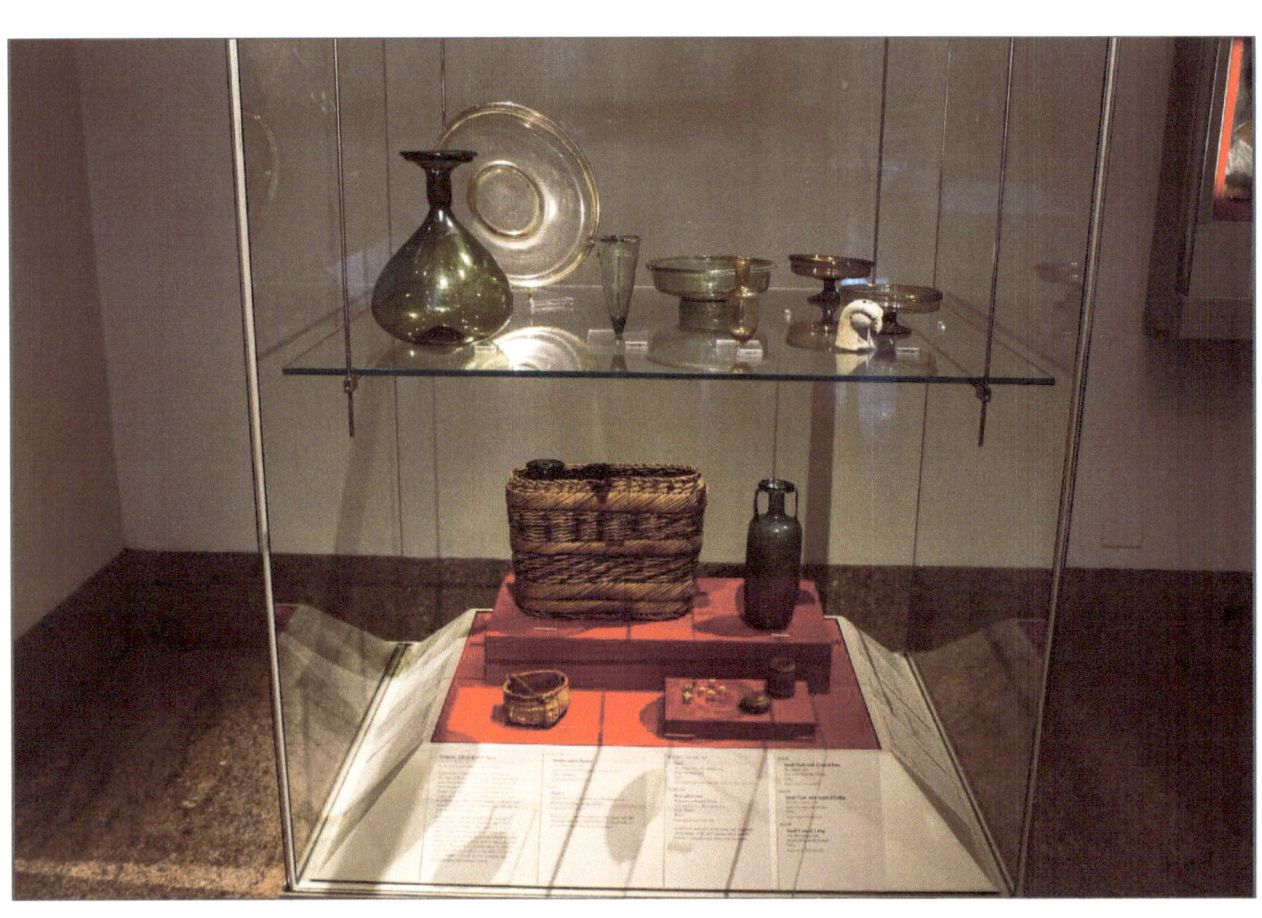

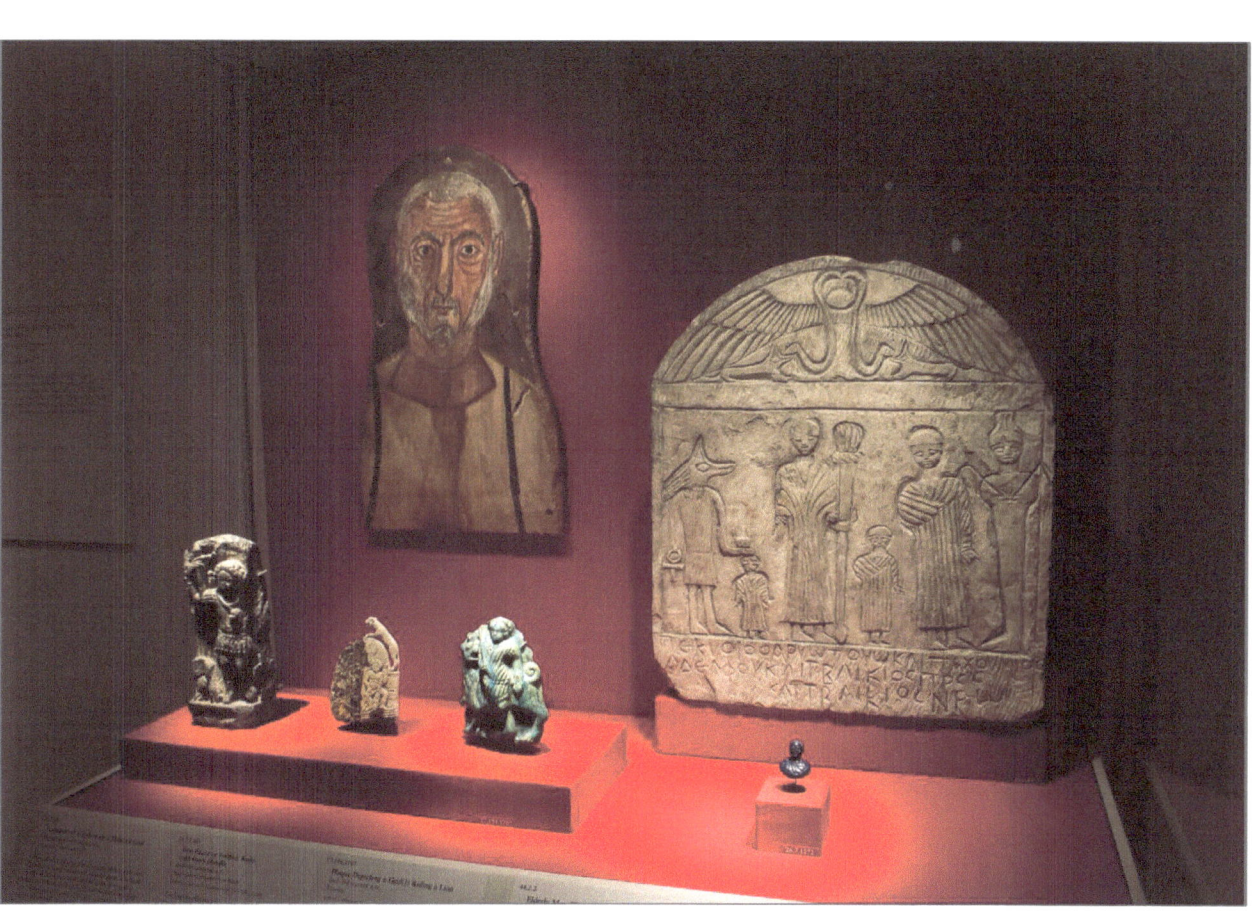

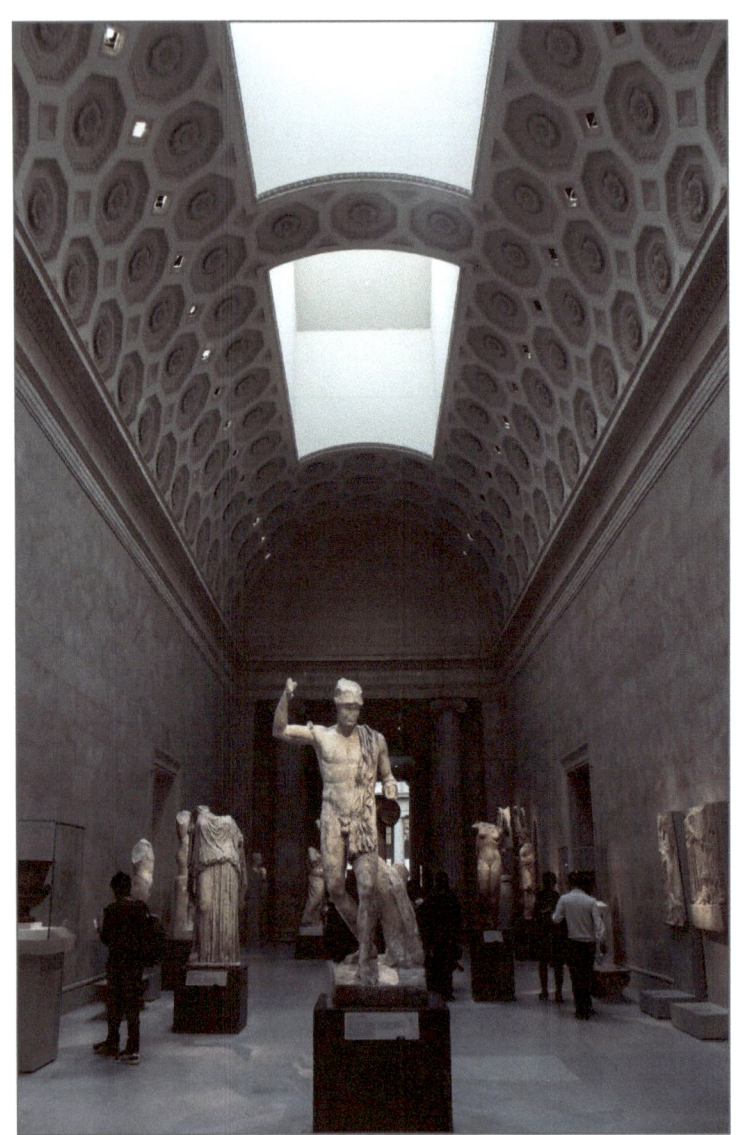

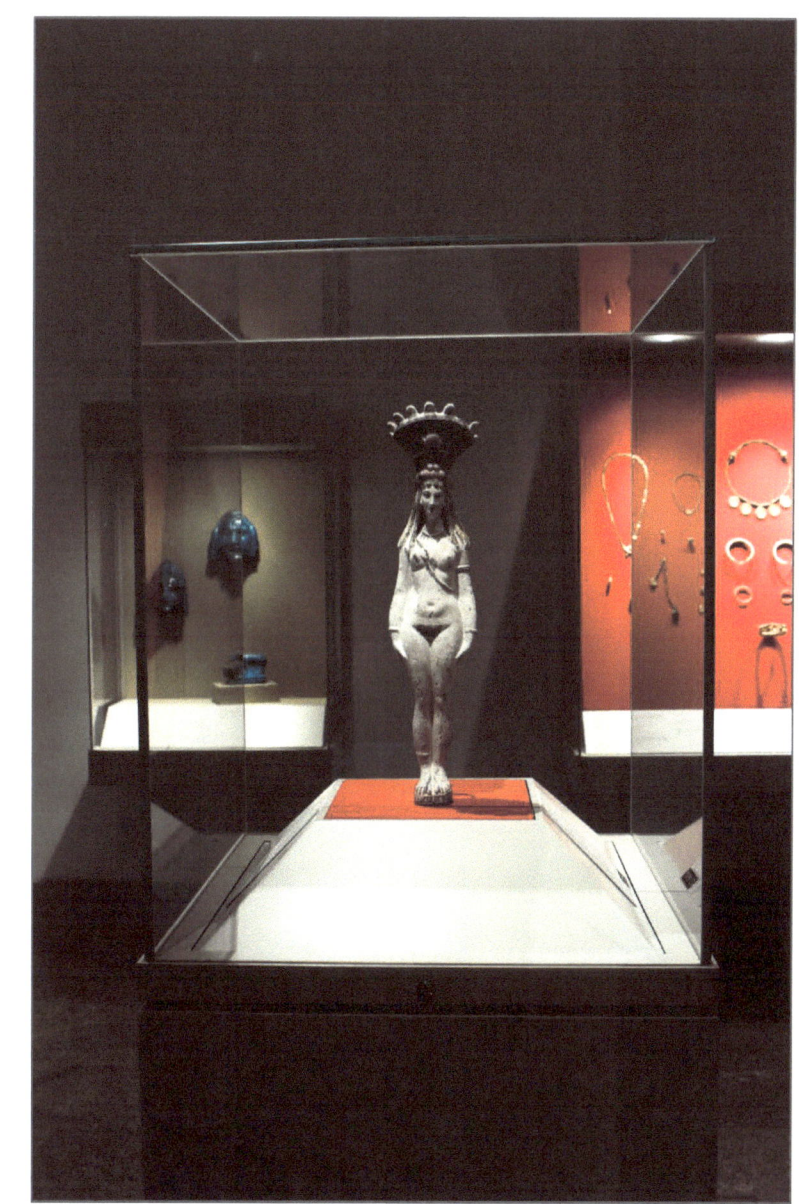

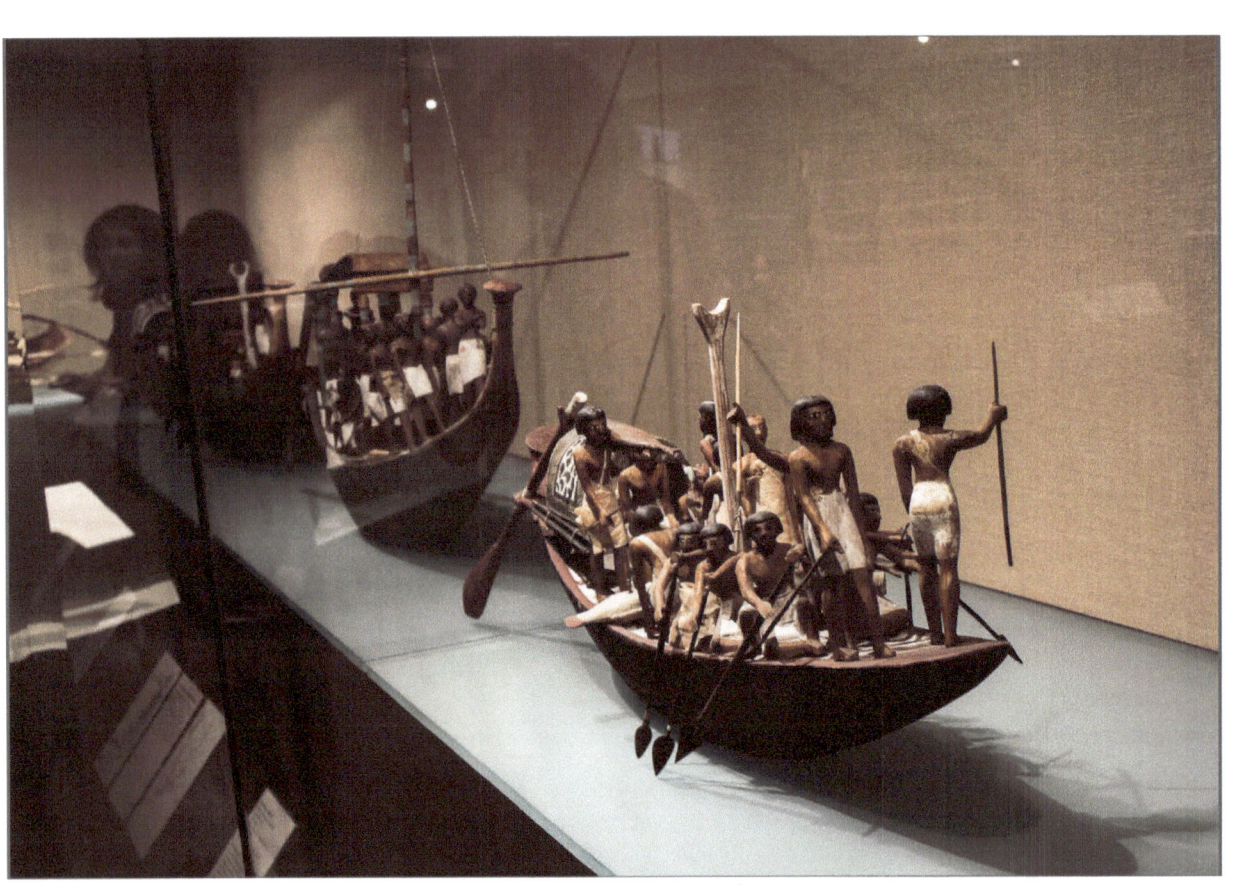

Sporting boat (X)

Dynasty 12, early reign of Amenemhat I
(ca. 1981–1975 B.C.)
Painted wood
Model chamber, tomb of Meketre (MMA 1101),
western Thebes

Rogers Fund and Edward S. Harkness Gift, 1920 (20.3.6)

Among the pleasures of an Egyptian noble's life were
hunting excursions in the Nile marshes. Papyrus rafts or
light boats such as this were used. Here, Meketre and his
son or companion are watching the hunters from a light
shelter made of woven reeds and decorated with two large
shields. In the prow, two men aim harpoons at some fish,
while amidships a kneeling fisherman removes the harpoon
from a bolti fish. An earlier catch, a large *Mormyrus*,
is being presented to Meketre. Birds already caught in
clapnets include bunches of coots presented by a man
and a duck held by a woman. The poles of the bird nets
are now lashed to the grilles of the shelter; the net pegs
lie on the deck. The presence of females from the noble's
family is the rule in marsh scenes. Besides other jewelry,
the young woman shown here wears a bead net over
her shoulders.

www.ingramcontent.com/pod-product-compliance
Lightning Source LLC
Chambersburg PA
CBHW050802180526
45159CB00004B/1527